Constance Wachtmeister, Kate Buffington Davis

Practical Vegetarian Cookery

Constance Wachtmeister, Kate Buffington Davis

Practical Vegetarian Cookery

ISBN/EAN: 9783744783545

Printed in Europe, USA, Canada, Australia, Japan

Cover: Foto ©Andreas Hilbeck / pixelio.de

More available books at **www.hansebooks.com**

PRACTICAL

VEGETARIAN COOKERY

EDITORS

The Countess Constance Wachtmeister
Kate Buffington Davis

"Thus the King's will is:
There hath been slaughter for the sacrifice
And slaying for the meat, but henceforth none
Shall spill the blood of life nor taste of flesh.
Seeing that knowledge grows, and life is one.
And mercy cometh to the merciful."

—*Light of Asia*.

FOR SALE BY

Mercury Pub. Co., 414 Mason St., San Francisco, Cal.
Theosophical Book Concern, 26 Van Buren St., Chicago, Ill.
Theosophical Pub. Co., 65 Fifth Ave., New York.
K. Buffington Davis, Minneapolis, Minn.
Theosophical Pub. Co., 26 Charing Cross, London, Eng.

Electrotyped by
The Printers Electrotyping Co.
Minneapolis, Minn.

INDEX.

PREFACE.

The aim of this book is to demonstrate the nutritious and appetising possibilities of vegetable foods. Cattle are becoming so diseased that apart from a humane revulsion against the consumption of meats in daily food, man is being driven for his own welfare to seek purer food substance. Any physical habit indulged in for generations is difficult to overcome, and the transition period between daily meat eating, and pure vegetarianism is a difficult one. We have endeavored to suggest such a variety of tasty and nutritious foods as will materially aid in making the change.

We do not claim this to be an exhaustive treatise on Vegetarian Cookery; only a clear and practical aid in the better preparations of some of the delicious products of the Vegetable Kingdom. Many children show a natural dislike to meats, and Mothers are at a loss how to supply them with proper nourishment when they reject the meat. Requests have come to us for aid through this very fact; and was one of the incentives to the bringing out of this book.

Mothers will have no difficulty in finding a plentiful variety of relishable and nutritious foods for the children if they will study the following pages. Equally easy will the formal dinner appear when one wishes to entertain Vegetarian friends.

INTRODUCTORY.

Vegetarianism from a Theosophical standpoint involves a whole philosophy of life. The short quotation on our title page well expresses the theosophic concept of the Unity of life, and the law of cause and effect which we call Karma. Life is fundamentally a unit, and aught that works ill to any manifestation thereof has effect on all. Through occult science we are taught a very practical lesson of direct benefit to the individual, by a diet free from blood. As clearly stated in Annie Besant's manual on "Man and his Bodies," man molds these instruments of his will, or true self. These bodies are but instruments; in no sense the man himself; and these instruments or bodies are finely responsive to the operator, or true self, only as they are purified and harmonized. Gross foods, and gluttony make gross bodies, not only physical, but astral as well. For the astral bodies feed on the subtle emanations of the foods supplying nutriment to the physical encasement. If, through the consumption of meats we feed the astral on the emanations of blood or animal life, we intensify the gross desire-nature of the astral man, intensify the passional-nature, and at death, when the physical body is cast aside as a discarded garment, the dense, gross, astral body is held to corresponding planes in the realm of the astral;

thus the purgatory of the Roman church becomes a very real and uncomfortable experience. If, on the contrary, clean habits of life have purified the astral body, when it is liberated at the hour of death from the prison house of flesh it is not of the same degree of density as the lower astral planes, and it passes on to the sunlit meadows of that world and away from its slums.

Alcohol has also a most pernicious effect on the astral vehicle, and for that reason is eliminated from the food of the occultist. It is a great mistake to give to the perishing, alcohol, or narcotics, as it has really a more serious effect on the out-going astral than on the physical encasement. When man learns to live on clean food, to have clean habits and to think clean, generous thoughts, there is naught in all this wonderful universe that he need fear.

VEGETARIAN COOKERY.

SOUPS.

SOUP STOCK.

Any nuts with herbs dried and ground will nicely flavor and enrich stock.

STOCK FOR CLEAR SOUPS.

Place four onions in large kettle with a gallon of water, let boil steadily two hours, then add one carrot, two small turnips, two parsnips, three bay leaves, one head of celery (if celery leaves cannot be had a saltspoonful of celery seeds may be used), one-eighth head of cabbage. Let boil four hours; strain. This should make a gallon of strong stock.

TOMATO BOUILLON.

Put one quart of tomatoes, with one and a half quarts of water, in kettle over the fire; add one tablespoonful of chopped onion, two bay leaves, four whole cloves, one level teaspoonful of celery seed and a half teaspoonful of pepper. Cover and cook twenty minutes. Strain through a sieve. Beat the whites of two eggs until partly light, add them to the tomato, and boil rapidly for five minutes. Strain through two thicknesses of cheese cloth. Re-heat, season with two teaspoonfuls of salt and serve with croutons.

JULIENNE SOUP.

Boil tender, not soft, one small potato, one small carrot, one half cupful of green peas (canned peas can be used), and one small head of celery, if in season; if in summer, asparagus heads will do. Cut the large vegetables into small dice, and add one quart of the clear stock. Take the yolks of two eggs, whipping them up with one tablespoonful of milk with salt to taste, put in a crockery cup and set in steamer; let cook until solid; set away to chill, then cut in small dice or fancy shapes and add to the soup.

MACARONI SOUP.

One-third package of Macaroni, or Spighetti; cook in boiling water, salted to taste, until tender, then drain quickly and add one quart of clear stock. Bring to a boiling point and serve.

TORONTO BISQUE.

Place a sauce pan, with half a cupful of fine chopped onion, the same of carrot and celery, over the fire; cover with boiling water; cook five minutes; drain off the water. Melt one tablespoonful of butter in a saucepan, add the parboiled vegetables; cover and cook ten minutes, stirring often; then add one heaping teaspoonful of flour, stir and cook two minutes, add one cupful of canned tomatoes, and one quart of boiling water, cook fifteen minutes. Shortly before serving rub the bisque through a sieve; mix the yolk of two eggs with half a cupful of cream; add it to the bisque, and stir for a few minutes over the fire. In the meantime cook two ounces of macaroni in salted water thirty-five minutes; drain and rinse it off with cold water; cut the macaroni into small pieces the size of a white bean; add one cupful of this macaroni to the bisque and serve.

TOMATO SOUP.

To one can of tomatoes add one pint of water, four peppercorns, one half bay leaf, four cloves, and a bit of mace; cook until the tomatoes are soft enough to strain. After straining add two teaspoonfuls of sugar, one teaspoonful of salt, one fourth teaspoonful of soda; thicken with two tablespoonfuls of butter and three tablespoonfuls of flour blended together.

CREAM OF TOMATO.

To one half can of tomatoes, add one scant tablespoonful of finely chopped onion, and three spikes of celery, cook until tender, then strain through a wire sieve; season to taste, add soda the size of a pea. Scald one quart of milk, mix one teaspoonful of butter with heaping teaspoonful of flour, dissolve in warm milk and stir into the scalding milk; add to the strained tomato stock just before serving; don't let it stand after milk is added. Serve with crackers.

DUTCH SOUP.

Take one bay leaf, one half can of tomatoes, one half can of corn, one medium sized onion, chopped; two heads of celery, cut fine (or one half teaspoonful of celery seed); one half cupful of rice, one half cupful of oatmeal, one carrot, cut in dice, one eighth head of cabbage, cut fine, one small turnip, cut fine, gallon, or more, of cold water, with salt to taste. Cook gently until all vegetables are thoroughly tender. Very nice served plain, or with dumplings. This soup is a hearty luncheon in itself.

CREAM OF POTATO.

To one head of celery, cut fine, add one teaspoonful of chopped onion, one large, or two medium sized potatoes, sliced; cook until you can mash through a wire sieve; then add one quart of scalding milk, one half cupful of cream, and thicken to a cream with buttered flour. Serve with oyster crackers.

POTATO SOUP WITH DUMPLINGS.

Pare, wash, and cut into dice, six good sized potatoes, chop fine one onion, place in kettle with water to cover, salt to taste, and cook until tender; then add one quart of cream or rich milk, add one tablespoonful of butter, a dash of pepper, and let come to a boil.

Have ready dumplings made as follows: To four heaping tablespoonfuls of flour add pinch of salt, one even teaspoonful baking powder, one tablespoonful cream, and water enough to make soft dough; do not knead, mould into small lumps, size of walnuts, and drop into soup as soon as the soup comes to a boil. The dumplings take about eight minutes to cook, and the kettle should be kept covered all the time. The soup needs to be carefully watched that it does not boil over or burn; it is well to lift the kettle free from the stove every three or four minutes, giving it a little twirl, but do not lift the cover until the eight minutes are passed, for sudden reduction of temperature may make the dumplings heavy.

RICE POTATO SOUP.

To two tablespoonfuls of rice, thoroughly washed, add one potato cut in large dice, one tablespoonful of finely chopped onion, and one-third of a teaspoonful of celery seed; cook until tender, salt to taste, add one quart of hot milk and one half cupful of cream. Serve with crackers.

SOUP WITH NOUILLES.

Nouilles—Beat two eggs, mix to a stiff paste with flour and a pinch of salt, roll out very thin on well floured board, let dry a few minutes, then roll snugly, cut from end of roll in strips as thin as possible, and shake out thoroughly. Have one quart clear stock hot and shake nouilles in gently. Let it simmer until nouilles are tender.

BEAN PURÉE WITH NOUILLES.

Take one pint of cold Boston baked beans; place in kettle with two quarts of water, one small onion, chopped fine, one small bay leaf; let boil until onion is tender, put through a wire strainer (if too thick, more water can be added); season to taste, add nouilles and let simmer until they are tender.

BEAN PURÉE WITH TOMATO.

To one bowl of cold Boston baked beans, add one half onion, chopped; one half teaspoonful of celery seed, one pint of tomatoes, one bay leaf, and one quart of water. Let boil one half hour, then mash through a colander, if too thick add more water, have ready one heaping teaspoonful of flour blended smooth with water, stir into the strained mixture, and put soup back on the fire, letting it come to a good boil. The flour is added to keep the soup an even creamy thickness. Serve with croutons.

RED KIDNEY BEAN SOUP.

To one can of red kidney beans, cooked in their own juice and then mashed through a seive to remove skins, add one quart of rich fresh milk, one tablespoonful of butter, salt and pepper to taste. Let come to a boil and serve with croutons, or wafers.

BLACK BEAN SOUP.

Soak a pint of black beans in two quarts of cold water over night; boil them four hours or more; mash them thoroughly, strain them through a colander into a saucepan, cover, and let boil. Mix a tablespoonful of flour smoothly with cold milk or cream, stir into the boiling soup until it thickens; add a cupful of butter; if it is too thick, thin with boiling water; add a tablespoonful of lemon juice. Season and spice to taste.

SPLIT PEA SOUP.

Put a pint of split peas, and one bay leaf, with two quarts of cold water in a covered saucepan to boil for four hours; mash the peas thoroughly, strain them through a colander into a saucepan; set it, covered, over the fire to boil; mix one tablespoonful of flour with a cupful of soft butter, stir it into the boiling soup until it thickens; cover and boil five minutes or more. If the soup is too thick it may be thinned with boiling water. Season to taste. One pint of strained tomato added to this makes a very nice soup, of different flavor.

CREAM OF CELERY.

Cut the tops of one stalk of celery; simmer gently until tender in sufficient water to cover, with one teaspoonful salt. Cut up celery stocks in one inch pieces and boil in one pint of water until tender. Boil two tablespoonfuls rice in water until nearly done; then add to the celery soup to boil a few minutes; strain celery tops and add the liquor to the soup pot. Boil one quart of milk in double boiler; thicken with one scant tablespoonful of flour blended with one tablespoonful of butter; add another teaspoonful of salt; add this to soup and let boil but a second. Have ready one half cupful of whipped cream; place in the bottom of the tureen, pour on the hot soup, and serve with crackers.

WHITE SOUP.

Put in a saucepan one and one half pint of water; when boiling throw in the white part of a cauliflower separated into sprays, let boil twenty minutes; then add bread balls made thus:—to one pint of bread crumbs, add powdered marjoram, thyme, sweet savory and chopped parsley, to taste; one tablespoonful of melted butter, pinch of salt, a little whole wheat flour and beaten egg to bind; form into little balls, size of walnuts, and drop into the soup and boil ten minutes; then add one pint of rich milk or cream to soup, and let come to a boil. Grate in a bit of cheese, just enough to flavor delicately. Serve with croutons.

CREAM OF CORN.

To one can of corn add three pints of milk; boil for half an hour. To one tablespoonful of chopped onion, add two tablespoonfuls of butter and cook in frying pan until delicate brown, then add to onion and butter two tablespoonfuls of flour; blend. Stir this mixture into the corn and milk; add salt and pepper to taste; cook five minutes; then run through coarse sieve to strain, and stir in the well beaten yolks of two eggs and one quarter of a cupful of cream; return to double boiler and cook until it thickens; do not let it boil.

CORN CHOWDER.

Pare and slice one large potato and one onion; place in agate kettle a layer of onion; cover that with one cupful of corn; then add the sliced potatoes; add just enough water to cover, and let simmer gently until onion and potatoes are tender. Add one quart of rich milk, one third cupful of cream and let come to a boil. Remove from fire and stir in the whipped yolk of one egg, and add a tablespoonful of chopped parsley.

GREEN PEA SOUP.

Put a quart of freshly shelled, unwashed peas into a double boiler, steam until the peas can be thoroughly mashed, pour in a quart of boiling milk, let boil for one minute and strain it through a colander into a saucepan; mix two tablespoonfuls of flour smoothly with cold milk; stir it into the boiling soup until it thickens; add two tablespoonfuls of butter, set it covered on the range, to boil five minutes or more,—until the flour is cooked. Season to taste. A sprig of mint cooked with the peas gives a flavor liked by many.

CABBAGE SOUP.

Steam a whole cabbage with the stem end down, for two hours or more, set it off, covered, to cool; take off the coarse outer leaves, chop the cabbage very fine, put it into a saucepan with a cupful of butter, and season to taste. Set it over the fire for the butter to melt; then dredge in gradually four tablespoonfuls of flour; stir, to mix it with the butter and cabbage, pour in a quart or more of boiling milk, or water, stir until it thickens; cover it and boil five minutes or more, to cook the flour.

CAULIFLOWER SOUP.

May be made the same as cabbage soup; only substituting cauliflower for cabbage.

CREAM OF ASPARAGUS.

Cut off half inch tips from two bunches asparagus stalks. Cook the stalks until tender in boiling water. Rub through a colander, salt to taste; add three pints of boiling milk; smooth one teaspoonful of butter with one of flour and stir into the soup. Cook fifteen minutes; while this is in course of preparation boil the tips till tender, drain and put in tureen. When soup is done take from stove, add one half cupful of cream and pour over the tips. Serve with croutons.

SUMMER VEGETABLE SOUP.

Pare two medium sized onions and one turnip, place these with one cupful of finely chopped cabbage to cook in three quarts of boiling water. Season to taste with salt and cook till tender, then add one cupful of green corn, cut from cob, bring to a quick boil and cook five minutes, add one half cupful of cream just before serving.

BLACK BEAN SOUP.

Soak one quart of black beans over night; put them in a kettle with a gallon of cold water and two bay leaves; boil slowly until well done, rub through a colander, and return to the kettle; season with salt, white pepper, and, if liked, a little thyme; blend one tablespoonful of butter with one tablespoonful of flour and dissolve in one half cupful of warm water; stir into the soup. Serve with croutons.

CARROT SOUP.

Boil six carrots in water; when thoroughly done drain them and pass them through a fine sieve. Mix the pulp thus obtained with as much clear stock (water will answer, but the soup will not be so good) as will make it of the desired consistency. Add pepper, salt, and a pinch of sugar. Melt one ounce of butter and mix with it a tablespoonful of flour; then gradually add to the carrot puree; let it come to a boil, add a small piece of butter; serve with croutons.

MOCK TURTLE SOUP.

Boil a bay leaf and a scant cupful of lentils in salted water until tender. Mash through colander to remove husks. Put back in kettle and add water enough to make one quart of soup; blend one table-spoonful of butter with scant tablespoonful of flour and stir into the soup; let come to a boil. Just before serving add fine slices of lemon, and two sliced, hard boiled, eggs.

SCOTS BROTH.

Wash two ounces of barley; soak it for three hours; chop one half of a medium sized head of cabbage, and one onion, put over to boil with the soaked barley, in one quart of water; salt to taste. Let boil for two hours; adding more water if it becomes too thick, be careful not to add too much water; season with savory herbs, or soup powder; add a tablespoonful of butter, and serve with croutons.

WHITE TURNIP SOUP.

Peel and prepare turnips according to quantity of soup desired, put them over to cook in boiling water; when half done add one fifth as much of onions, chopped very fine, with pepper and salt to taste. When turnips are tender pour the liquid through a sieve and rub the turnips through with a spoon. Return to kettle and add as much milk as is required to bring soup to the proper consistency; add a little parsley, chopped fine; one cupful of cream, and one tablespoonful of butter blended with one teaspoonful of flour. Serve with croutons.

CREAM OF LIMA BEANS.

Soak one cupful of dried lima beans over night; in the morning drain and add three pints of cold water. Cook until tender and rub through a sieve. Cut two slices of onion and four slices of carrot into small cubes; cook in two tablespoonfuls of butter until yellow, add one cupful of cream or milk, two tablespoonfuls of butter, two tablespoonfuls of flour, one teaspoonful of salt, and one saltspoonful of pepper; and stir into the boiling soup.. Strain and serve.

BEAN PUREE WITH TOMATO.

To one pint of cold Boston baked beans, add one chopped, small, onion, one bay leaf, and one cupful of tomato; boil in one quart of water until tender, then mash through a colander, put back in kettle over the fire and add one tablespoonful of butter blended with one teaspoonful of flour; season to taste, let come to a boil, and serve with croutons.

SAVORIES AND RELISHES.

SAVORY HASH.

Take one third of brown lentils (which have been cooked tender and rubbed through colander) to two thirds of chopped cold boiled potatoes, add one cupful of bread crumbs over which has been poured one tablespoonful of melted butter. Season, adding savory, soup powder or sage and chopped onion, as preferred; put tablespoonful of butter in frying pan, add the hash, cover until thoroughly heated, then remove cover and let brown, turn out on platter garnished with parsley.

NUT LOAF.

Grind or chop very fine one half pound of nuts—any kind you prefer; add one pound of broken bread, one fourth pound of butter; turn on one pint of boiling water and one egg, well beaten, salt, pepper, and sage to taste; chop very fine. Butter a pudding dish, cover the buttered surface with bread crumbs, pour in the mixture, and bake one hour or until well done. Turn out on a platter, garnish with parsley or celery tops. Serve with cranberry sauce.

VEGETABLE SWEET BREADS.

To six tablespoonfuls of lentils, previously boiled in salted water until tender and mashed through a colander, add three tablespoonfuls of bread crumbs and two beaten eggs, mix well together and fry by tablespoonfuls in plenty of hot butter. Serve hot, with green peas.

STUFFED SQUASH.

Boil or steam, a good sized summer squash, it needs to be of tender skin, leave on the skin and cut it once across before putting on to cook; let it cook until tender, be careful not to break in taking up; scoop out the seeds with a spoon, have ready some bread crumbs in which have been mixed one tablespoonful of melted butter and tablespoonful of finely minced onion and an equal quantity of chopped parsley or mint, as you prefer, with salt and pepper to taste; fill the cavity in squash with this stuffing and fasten together. Place in the oven and bake one half hour, basting frequently with butter and hot water.

STUFFED CUCUMBERS.

Take three medium sized cucumbers, pare, remove the seed centers and fill with stuffing. Bind the halves together with tape and steam until tender; remove all tapes, but one, that through the middle, lay them in a baking dish and brush them over with egg; then scatter fine bread crumbs and brown. Serve in long dish, with brown gravy.

The stuffing is made as follows: Put one tablespoonful of melted butter in stew pan, fry in the butter until brown one onion and two medium sized

apples chopped fine. Drain from the fat and make
into stuffing with bread crumbs flavored with a little
mint, savory, or sage, as one prefers; whip one egg
and stir in, with seasoning to taste.

VEGETABLE CUTLETS.

Use as a basis the vegetables from which the clear
soup stock is made; after they have been thoroughly
drained, set away, and chilled they will chop nicely
without mushing. To the quantity of vegetables used
for one gallon of soup stock, add one half can of peas,
and one quart of chopped, cold, boiled potatoes; pepper and salt to taste. Mould in flat cutlet shapes,
dip in fine bread crumbs, then in egg, again in bread
crumbs, and fry in hot oil or butter. Serve hot. This
will make about four dozen cutlets. If the chopped
vegetables are placed in a cool place they will keep
nicely several days.

CELERY ON TOAST.

After washing and removing green leaves, cut celery stocks into pieces about four inches long and cook
in boiling, salted, water; when tender, lay on buttered
toast, moistened with the water the celery was cooked
in; add a brown sauce, and serve.

TURNIP SOUFFLÉ.

Make a white sauce of three tablespoonfuls of butter, three of flour, and enough milk to make a thick,
white sauce; use three cupfuls of strained cooked
turnip, whites of three well beaten eggs, a tea-

spoonful finely chopped onion; salt, and a dash of cayenne; mix all together, adding the whites of eggs last folding them carefully in, bake in a well buttered pan in slow oven until a delicate brown.

FARINA CROUSTADES.

Put one quart of water in double boiler and add one teaspoonful of salt; when scalding hot stir in gradually one and one half cupful of farina; let it cook till very thick; then spread out on a flat buttered dish about one and one half inches thick; when perfectly cold cut with a round cutter and scoop out some of the center so as to make a sort of cup; brush over with the yolk of egg and set in oven till a delicate brown.

For filling, cut into dice, three hard boiled eggs, season with salt, cayenne, and chopped parsley; add two tablespoonfuls of mushrooms cut in half; mix with enough well seasoned brown sauce to moisten well; fill the litle croustades and serve; pass more of the filling or sauce in a gravy boat.

RICE CROQUETTES.

One cupful of rice, boiled in one pint of milk and one of water until tender. While boiling, add butter the size of an egg, two teaspoonfuls of sugar, three eggs, and the juice and grated peel of one lemon. Mix well, make into rolls a finger long, and dip first into yolks of two eggs, well beaten, then into cracker crumbs, and fry in hot cocoanut butter.

ITALIAN MACARONI.

Boil one third of a package of Macaroni in salted water until tender, drain and rinse in cold water; heat and cover with tomato sauce (see sauces and gravies).

MACARONI PIE.

Boil a quarter of a pound of macaroni in water until quite soft; pour off the water; add half a pint of milk, a quarter of a pound of grated cheese, a piece of butter, a very little mustard, salt, a pinch of cayenne, and a dust of white pepper. Let it boil for a minute, then bake in a dish lined with rich crust. The crust should be brushed with the white of egg to keep it dry.

MACARONI CHEESE.

Take the quantity of macaroni required to fill a baking dish two thirds full, and boil until tender in salted water, drain through a colander and rinse in cold water, place in baking dish with half a cupful of milk if quantity used is small, a whole cupful if two quart dish is to be filled, add cupful of grated cheese, pinch of soda and dash of cayenne; bake a delicate brown.

VEGETABLE HOT-POT.

Use one turnip, one Spanish onion, one cupful of stewed tomato, one and one half pound of potatoes; one half cupful of tapioca previously soaked, butter, pepper, and salt to taste. Cut turnip into dice and boil until tender, at the same time let tapioca cook clear. Cut potatoes up fine, and chop onion fine and scald. Place a layer of onion at bottom of buttered baking dish, then tapioca, on top of this, potatoes, chopped turnip, and tomato,—with a little butter on each layer; repeat this until the dish is full, and have a layer of potatoes at the top. Bake in hot oven for one hour, the last quarter remove cover; add layer of bread crumbs and brown.

WINTER VEGETABLE PIE.

Place in baking dish, slices of cold boiled potatoes, onions, celery, and carrot, then add one scant cupful of stewed tomatoes and one half can of peas. Cover with stock, thickened to a gravy with butter and flour, cover with plain crust, and bake. A pie of this nature can be made with a great variety of ingredients; apples, boiled chestnuts, onions, and potatoes make a good combination. Rice, with a grating of cheese, celery, onion, and tomato, another variety.

VEGETABLE HASH.

Of cooked and chopped vegetables, use one carrot, one blood beet, two turnips, two quarts of finely sliced potatoes, one onion, and a stalk of celery; one sprig of parsley; put them in a stew pan, cover tight, and set in the oven. When thoroughly heated pour over a gravy of drawn butter and cream. Stir together and serve.

NUT CROQUETTES.

Shell and grind one pound of English walnuts, add one teaspoonful of salt, and the juice of half a lemon, one tablespoonful of chopped parsley, a dash of cayenne pepper; mix thoroughly. Place one cupful of milk in double boiler; rub one tablespoonful of softened butter with two tablespoonfuls of flour; when the cream is hot, stir in the flour and butter; cook until it thickens; season lightly.

Then turn the thickened cream into the nut mixture; have ready a well beaten egg and whip in; mix all together thoroughly. Set away to cool; when cold form into shapely rolls, dip in bread crumbs, then in beaten egg, again in bread crumbs, and fry quickly in hot fat. Be sure the fat is at right temperature.— see "Important Notes."

BISCUIT PATES.

Make a nice light baking powder biscuit. Have ready, when the biscuits are done, one cupful of small mushrooms cooked tender and cut fine, dressed with one half cupful of cream, mixed with juice of mushrooms, and thickened with one teaspoonful of flour, blended with teaspoonful of butter; season to taste with salt and pepper. Take a thin slice off of the bottom of the biscuit, dig out the center, leaving reasonably thick walls, put little piece of butter in the shell and fill with mushrooms dressing; serve at once. Stale biscuit may be used by toasting them a few minutes in a hot oven after they have been hollowed out. These are crisp and some prefer them to fresh biscuit.

YORKSHIRE PUDDING.

To six large tablespoonfuls of flour, add one teaspoonful of baking powder and one half teaspoonful of salt; sift thoroughly; beat the yolks of three eggs. and add milk enough to mix with flour and make the consistency of soft custard; whip whites of eggs to stiff froth and fold into mixture lightly. Melt a heaping tablespoonful of butter in dripping pan, letting it brown slightly; pour in the mixture and place in oven; then pour over the top a half cupful of melted butter; brown another spoonful of butter, and when pudding is almost done baste with browned butter. When done cut in squares and serve with melted butter.

FRIED APPLES.

Wash apples and dry them, cut in circular slices through the core of the apples. Sprinkle liberally with sugar and fry in butter until well cooked. Serve on a platter.

VEGETABLE SAUSAGES NO. 1.

Take three cupfuls of grated bread crumbs and moisten with hot water; add salt, pepper, and mixed herbs. Beat till light, one egg and add to bind. Shape in small cakes, or rolls, and fry in hot grease.

SAUSAGES NO. 2.

Take one cupful of boiled, or Boston baked, beans; heat, and mash through seive; chop two onions and boil very tender, mash, and add to beans. Place in oven one cupful of bread crumbs and let them dry and brown, then roll to powder; add to the mixture, bind with an egg, and use savory or sage to flavor, with salt and pepper to season. Roll in shape, dip in wheat meal, and brown in hot butter or oil.

CHINESE RICE.

Wash rice thoroughly, have agate kettle half filled with boiling salted water. Sprinkle rice in the boiling water; let cook until rice is thoroughly tender; then drain through a sieve.

CURRIED RICE WITH EGGS.

Prepare Chinese rice and serve with curried gravy made as follows: Put one teaspoonful of chopped onion in frying pan, with one heaping tablespoonful of butter; thicken with browned flour and add sufficient water to make gravy of right consistency. Season with salt, pepper, and curry powder enough to delicately flavor. Heap rice in center of shallow dish, or platter, pour the gravy around the edge of rice, garnish with slices of hard boiled eggs, and lemon.

BANANA FRITTERS.

Slice bananas one half inch thick; squeeze over the slices some orange juice; stand for fifteen minutes; drain each piece, dip in fritter batter and fry.

CURRIED RICE.

Thoroughly wash one cupful of rice; let soak several hours in cold water; put two tablespoonfuls of butter in saucepan; add one teaspoonful finely chopped onion; when the onion begins to color drain the rice and add to onion and butter; stir a few minutes; add two teaspoonfuls curry powder, salt and pepper; then add two and one half cupfuls of boiling water; cover and cook rapidly for ten minutes; then move where it will cook very slowly three quarters of an hour.

IRISH STEW.

Chop fine a small onion, put over to stew in one pint of water; add a bay leaf and half a teaspoonful of salt; let simmer until onion is tender, take out the bay leaf; add pint of milk and one large potato, pared and sliced thickly; let simmer until potato is tender, then add one spoonful of flour blended with half a teacupful of butter; add chopped three hard boiled eggs, pour over split baking powder biscuit and serve on a platter, garnished with parsley.

CHESTNUT CROQUETTES.

Boil one quart of the large French chestnuts; remove the shells and thin brown skin; mash and run through a sieve; put into a double boiler, add enough sugar to sweeten, about two tablespoonfuls, the grated peel of one orange and juice of one half of a lemon, one tablespoonful of finely chopped citron; beat the yolk of one egg with one tablespoonful of cream; add to the chestnuts; turn out and when perfectly cold, form into croquettes; dip in egg, then in bread crumbs or fine cake crumbs may be used; fry in deep hot fat.

For the sauce, put into a double boiler one half cupful of thick cream, three fourths cupful of strong coffee, three tablespoonfuls of sugar and the yolks of four eggs well beaten; stir till it begins to thicken, remove from the fire; add juice of one half an orange, one tablespoonful of lemon juice, three teaspoonfuls Maraschino; serve with the croquettes.

MUSHROOMS.

GRILLED MUSHROOMS.

Prepared in this way the mushrooms must be large. After washing and peeling, score the tops with a knife and lay them for one hour in a pickle of oil, salt, pepper and lemon juice. Place them, tops down, on a close-barred gridiron and broil over a clear, slow fire. Serve on toast with a sauce made as follows:

Chop the stalks and pieces of mushrooms that have broken in the washing and stew in broth for ten minutes with a little minced parsley and onion. Beat the yolk of one egg with a gill of cream and add slowly to the sauce. Stir the whole until hot without boiling and pour it over the toast.

ESCALOPED MUSHROOMS.

Put the mushrooms in a buttered baking-dish with alternate layers of crumbs, seasoning each layer plentifully with butter; add salt, pepper and a gill of cream or gravy. Bake twenty minutes, keeping covered while in the oven.

MUSHROOM PIE.

Line a baking dish with rich crust. Drain the liquor from a can of small mushrooms, slice the mushrooms, add one cupful of cream, or rich milk, and tablespoonful of butter, to juice of mushrooms. Season to taste and thicken with tablespoonful of flour blended with butter; add the mushrooms, fill in the baking dish, cover with top crust and bake a rich brown. Brown sauce may be used if preferred.

AUNT SUSAN'S MUSHROOM PIE.

Line a deep pudding pan with rich paste; fill two thirds full of mushrooms (if raw they must be stewed a few minutes first), make a gravy of flour rubbed very smooth with thick cream, or with butter and milk, thin with boiling water, season with salt, pepper and soup powder, pour over the mushrooms, cover with paste and bake.

BAKED MUSHROOMS.

Toast for each person a large slice of bread and spread over with rich sweet cream; lay on each slice, head downward, a mushroom, or if small, more than one; season and fill each with as much cream as it will hold. Place over each a custard cup, pressing well down to the toast; set in a moderate oven and cook fifteen minutes. Do not remove the cups for five minutes after they come from the oven, as thereby the flavor of the mushroom is preserved in its entirety.

STEWED MUSHROOMS.

Drain off the juice from a can of small mushrooms; put a heaping tablespoonful of butter into a frying pan; add two tablespoonfuls of flour and brown well, stirring all the time; then pour in the juice of mushrooms with water enough to make a thin gravy; season with salt, pepper, and soup powder; add mushrooms and stew a few minutes, then serve.

MUSHROOMS IN WHITE SAUCE.

For stewing, the smaller mushrooms are preferable. Carefully peel the tops, cut the ends of the stalks level, wash and drain in colander. They should be stewed, till tender, in as little water as possible. When thoroughly cooked, add a pint of cream, or new milk, and thicken in usual way with flour blended in melted butter.

MUSHROOMS WITH LEMON.

Use the small canned mushrooms, separate the mushrooms from the liquor, put them, with one tablespoonful of butter in saucepan; add one tablespoonful of lemon juice, a pinch of white pepper, and one quarter of a teaspoonful of salt; place the saucepan over a slow fire and cook gently fifteen minutes, then serve

EGGS.

CURRIED EGGS, NO. 1.

Put into saucepan two tablespoonfuls of butter, add one half teaspoonful onion juice; cook slowly till the onion begins to color; then add one tablespoonful flour and one teaspoonful curry powder; when perfectly smooth add three fourths of a cupful of clear stock and one half cupful of cream; cook for five minutes, stirring constantly; season with salt and pepper. Cut six hard boiled eggs into halves lengthwise; strain the sauce over them and let stand on the stove a few minutes till thoroughly heated. Serve on thin squares of toast.

CURRIED EGGS, NO. 2.

Boil half a dozen eggs hard and let them get cold. Fry in butter two large onions cut in thin slices, and let them get quite brown, season these with pepper and salt, and add a pint of boiling water; when the onions have stewed for a little while, put in a cupful of milk thickened with arrowroot, or flour, and flavor with curry powder, let it simmer, then put in the eggs cut in halves, making them hot, but do not let them boil. The amount of curry powder used is a matter of taste; garnish the dish with boiled rice, and serve very hot.

BAKED EGGS.

Butter gem pans and line with fine, buttered, bread crumbs. Break one egg carefully into each pan, season with bits of pepper, salt and butter, cover lightly with buttered bread crumbs, and bake in oven until delicate brown.

SCRAMBLED EGGS.

Break the eggs into a bowl and beat moderately light; add cream in proportion of one tablespoonful to every two eggs; season to taste. Have one tablespoonful of butter melted in hot frying pan and pour into the mixture. Stir until cooked solid, turn on hot platter and serve at once with toast.

SHIRRED EGGS.

Set a saucer on the stove—the heavy japanese ware stands the heat best—and put in it a teaspoonful of butter, when hot break two eggs into the dish, let cook until they bubble, and begin to set. Serve in the dish in which they are cooked, slipping the saucer on to a small plate. Serve at once.

HARD BOILED EGGS.

The eggs should be placed in boiling water, then set where they will simmer, rather than boil, and be left for fifteen minutes; the yolks will be dry and fine. To make them peel easily slip at once into cold water on removing from the fire.

LYONNAISE EGGS.

Put one half tablespoonful butter in sauce pan, add one teaspoonful onion juice, cook slowly five minutes. Add one tablespoonful flour and, when well mixed, add one and one half cupfuls milk, stir till it thickens, season with salt and pepper, pour the sauce in a bake-dish, and break six eggs onto the sauce. Sprinkle quite thickly with bread crumbs, put bits of butter over all, and set in the oven for three or four minutes.

EGGS WITH MUSHROOMS.

Trim and peel the mushrooms; put them in stew-pan with butter, and cook until tender, season to taste. Place in shallow dish pouring the butter over them, then break over them eggs enough to cover, sprinkle thickly with bread crumbs and add bits of butter, place in hot oven long enough to set the eggs. Do not let the eggs harden; four or five minutes is the time usually required. Serve at once.

SAVORY EGGS.

Fry slices of Spanish onions until a delicate brown; add a tablespoonful of chopped parsley, pepper and salt, blend fat with tablespoonful of flour; add a pint of hot milk. Have ready some hard boiled eggs, quarter, and heat in the prepared sauce. Serve on toast.

FRICASSEED EGGS.

Boil the eggs till hard, take them out of the shells and arrange on a platter either in halves, or the yolks whole and whites cut in dice; make a rich white sauce and pour over them, garnish the dish with parsley.

EGGS FORCED.

Boil the number of eggs required; throw into cold water to chill; peel, and cut crosswise, take out the yolks, being careful not to break the whites. Rub the yolks with tablespoonful of butter (if six eggs are used), add two tablespoonfuls of cooked, chopped, mushrooms, pepper, salt, and one tablespoonful of chopped parsley; heat this mixture and beat it to a paste. Stuff with it the whites of the eggs and serve cold on bed of cress.

EGG CUTLETS.

For each cutlet allow one hard boiled egg, chopped fine, a tablespoonful of bread crumbs, the same quantity of grated cheese, a pinch of curry powder, pepper and salt; mix the whole with the beaten yolk of a raw egg and shape like cutlet; dip in white of egg and bread crumbs and fry brown; serve very hot.

ROASTED EGGS.

Fresh eggs well roasted are considered by some to be much richer than boiled eggs. Eggs may be roasted in the oven or in hot ashes. Care should be taken to turn them, where the heat is unequal.

EGGS IN CREAM.

Put half a cupful, or more, of cream into a shallow earthen dish, and place the dish in pan of boiling

water. When the cream is hot, break in as many eggs
as the bottom of the dish will hold, and cook until
well set, basting them occasionally over the top with
the hot cream, season to taste, and serve promptly.

ESCALOPED EGGS.

Boil six eggs fifteen minutes, the water should
simmer, rather than boil; then slip the eggs into cold
water for a moment, to make them peel easily, remove
the shells and set aside to cool. Make a white sauce
of rich milk thickened with butter and flour, seasoned
to taste. Remove the whites of eggs and chop; cream
the yolks with one half cupful of cream and add to
white souce. Stir in the chopped up whites, and add
a teaspoonful of chopped parsley; place in baking dish,
sprinkle bread crumbs and bits of butter over the top
and set in hot oven just long enough to brown delicately.

POACHED EGGS, SPANISH STYLE.

Heat an earthen pan slowly and melt in it a tablespoonful of butter; add a teaspoonful of salt, a
smaller quantity of pepper and a small onion minced
very fine; or in place of the onion, use parsley, and
sweet herbs, or a combination of all together as you
prefer. Drop in the eggs one at a time; do not stir,
but let them brown a little; turn carefully and brown
on the other side. In Spain and Mexico they are
served in the dish in which they are cooked, and as
hot as possible.

SWISS EGGS.

Cover the bottom of a dish with two ounces of fresh butter and on this scatter grated cheese; drop the eggs upon the cheese without breaking the yolks, season to taste. Pour over the eggs a little cream and sprinkle with about two ounces of grated cheese; set in a moderate oven for ten or fifteen minutes.

FRENCH OMELET (PLAIN).

Beat the yolks of six eggs to a cream, and beat whites to a stiff froth, add two tablespoonfuls of cream, or rich milk, to the yolks, season to taste, whip in the beaten whites lightly. Have omelet pan well oiled with butter and moderately hot; cook slowly until browned slightly on the bottom, then set pan in upper grate in hot oven. Serve on a platter garnished with parsley.

DRESSED OMELETS.

A nice variety can be given omelets by filling supplied just before folding.

TOMATO DRESSING.

Five tomatoes stewed down, and seasoned with salt, pepper and butter. Spread on omelet just before folding.

OMELET, WITH FRENCH PEAS.

Heat and drain one can of peas, season with salt, pepper and butter. Cover the platter and serve omelet on peas.

MUSHROOM FILLING.

If fresh mushrooms are used, select the small variety; peel and slice them, stew until tender in butter; season to taste and spread on omelet before folding.

FOAMY OMELET (SWEET).

Beat the yolks of six eggs to a cream, add one half cupful of cream, one tablespoonful of sugar. Whip the whites to a stiff froth, and add one half to the mixture; have frying pan moderately hot, melt one teaspoonful of butter in pan; be careful not to brown, and pour in the mixture. Cook carefully, lifting pan from fire frequently so it will not scorch on the bottom; when nearly set, pour over the rest of whites of eggs, and sprinkle with powdered sugar, then set in oven until whites of eggs set; have ready a hot platter, slip omelet on to platter, lay spoonfuls of jelly on omelet and double quickly. Serve at once. This omelet without sweetening is very nice with savory dressing, such as minced herbs heated in butter.

BREAD OMELET.

Crumble a cupful of stale bread and soak in half a teacupful of milk. Then beat quite smooth, and add half a teaspoonful of salt and five beaten eggs. Butter a shallow pudding dish well, pour in the mixture, and bake in an oven about ten minutes, serving at once in the same dish, as it falls quickly.

VEGETABLE OMELET.

Chop an onion finely, together with two crisp heads of lettuce, season with salt and pepper, and stir in six well beaten eggs, add three tablespoonfuls of cream. Pour into hot, buttered spider, and when thickened, but not hardened, fold over and serve on hot platter. Parsley may be used, if preferred, in place of lettuce.

CHEESE OMELET, NO. 1.

Break three eggs into a basin; whip them till well mixed; add pepper and salt, and two ounces of grated cheese; melt one tablespoonful of butter in frying pan; when the butter is quite hot pour the mixture into the pan; as soon as it begins to set, draw the thickening portion from the bottom of pan with a silver fork, letting the liquid substance cover the pan, do not stir; repeat this operation until it is all sufficiently cooked; then turn onto a heated platter, garnished with parsley, or cress.

CHEESE OMELET, NO. 2.

Mix to a smooth batter three tablespoonfuls of flour with half a pint of milk. Beat together four eggs, a little salt and one fourth of a pound of old cheese grated. Add these to the flour and milk and mix all, beating briskly for several minutes. Put three ounces of butter on a frying pan, and when it is boiling hot pour in the mixture and cook to a nice brown on both sides, turning carefully. Serve on a hot dish.

EGG AND ASPARAGUS.

Cut about two dozen stalks of asparagus into inch lengths and boil tender. Drain, pour over a cupful of drawn butter; stir until hot, turn into a baking dish. Break about six eggs on top, put a bit of butter on each, with salt, and pepper; put into a quick oven until the eggs are "set."

DEVILLED EGGS.

Boil the eggs for twenty minutes, remove the shells, cut each egg in half without breaking the whites; take out the yolks and pound them in a mortar, adding cayenne, salt and curry powder. Stuff the whites with this paste and join the eggs to their original shape. Cut off just sufficient of each broad end to enable them to stand, and arrange them thus on a dish in a bed of cress or parsley.

EGGS ON TOAST.

Put one tablespoonful of butter in a chaffing dish, and when bubbling add one tablespoonful of flour, one half teaspoonful of salt, one half saltspoonful of pepper, and, gradually, one cupful of milk. Add the whites of three hard boiled eggs, chopped fine. When hot, pour over three slices of toast. Rub the yolks through a strainer over all and garnish with parsley.

SAVORY SAUCES AND GRAVIES.

Nut butter is an excellent substitute for meat essence in gravies, stocks, and sauces. It should be used in the proportion of one tablespoonful to one quart of water.

BROWN SAUCE.

Heat a pint of thin cream; when boiling add a tablespoonful of flour, browned in the oven and rubbed to a smooth paste with a little cold milk; salt to taste; cook thoroughly for ten minutes; then add one cupful of hot, stewed, strained tomato. Beat thoroughly.

TOMATO SAUCE, NO. 1.

Melt one tablespoonful butter, add one tablespoonful of chopped onion, fry until delicate brown; then add one tablespoonful of flour; gradually pour in one cupful of clear soup stock and one half cupful of strained juice of tomato. Season to taste, and cook until it thickens. Nut or dairy butter may be used.

TOMATO SAUCE, NO. 2.

Put one half can of tomatoes, one cupful of water, two cloves, two alspice berries, two pepper corns, two sprigs of parsley, one teaspoonful of mixed herbs, over to boil in granite saucepan; fry one tablespoonful of chopped onion in one tablespoonful of butter till a delicate brown; then add tomato mixture and one heaping tablespoonful of corn starch that has been dissolved in cold water. Simmer ten minutes, add one half teaspoonful of salt, and one half saltspoonful of pepper, add a dash of cayenne, if liked. Strain.

WHITE SAUCE.

To one pint of milk add one heaping tablespoonful of flour blended with one tablespoonful of melted butter; boil until it thickens, salt to taste, add one half cupful of cream. If too thick, thin with hot milk.

CHEESE SAUCE.

Flavor white sauce by adding grated cheese, and stir until the cheese is quite melted.

DUTCH SAUCE.

To four ounces of butter add the well beaten yolks of three eggs, a teaspoonful of flour, a dessertspoonful of lemon juice and salt to taste; put in double boiler and stir gently until it thickens; do not let it boil or it will curdle. This sauce is very nice with asparagus or cauliflower.

DRAWN BUTTTER.

One half cupful of butter, rubbed well with two tablesponfuls of flour; put into saucepan with about one pint of boiling water, stir constantly until well melted. Add one tablespoonful of chopped parsley.

BUTTER SAUCE.

Season a cupful of flour with pepper, nutmeg, and cloves. Mix it with water into a thin paste, and work in a piece of butter about the size of an egg. Put the paste into a pan over the fire, and boil it for a quarter of an hour, then take it off, and add some fresh butter in small portions at a time, continually stirring the contents, to prevent the butter from rising to the surface. Afterwards add lemon juice to flavor, and mix thoroughly. This sauce may be used with almost any vegetable. Another way of making butter sauce sometimes called oiled butter, which is generally liked, is to take as much fresh butter as will be wanted, and melt it, but do not let it brown. Skim it, pour it out, let it rest a minute, then drain it from the curd at the bottom, and serve.

BROWN BUTTER GRAVY.

Take one bay leaf, and a teaspoonful of chopped onion and simmer fifteen minutes in one pint of water. Brown two tablespoonfuls of flour. Put one heaping tablespoonful of butter in frying-pan, melt, browning slightly, add flour, then the strained water that is flavored with onion and bay leaf; let boil, if too thick add more hot water. Salt and pepper to taste.

CHEESE DISHES.

AN ENGLISH MONKEY.

Soak one cupful of bread crumbs in one cupful of milk about ten or fifteen minutes. Melt one table-spoonful of butter, add one cupful of cheese broken into small pieces; stir until melted; add the crumbs and one beaten egg, one half teaspoonful of salt, a few grains of cayenne, and a piece of bicarbonate of soda as large as a pea. Cook for five minutes; serve on wafers.

RICE AND CHEESE.

Take one pint of boiled rice and one cupful of grated cheese; add to the cheese a dash of cayenne pepper and soda the size of a small pea; mix thoroughly. Place the rice and cheese in alternate layers in buttered baking dish. Sprinkle bits of butter over the top and bake in hot oven until brown.

WELSH RAREBIT.

Take one fourth pound of good rich cheese, grate it, add one half cupful of milk; put in a double boiler. Mix one half teaspoonful mustard, one saltspoonful of salt, a sprinkle of cayenne pepper and soda the size of a small pea, to a smooth paste with a little milk; add the yolks of two eggs, and beat well. When the cheese is melted stir in mixture of egg and seasoning, add two teaspoonfuls of butter, and cook until it thickens, stirring constantly. Pour over toast, or heated square crackers and serve at once.

CHEESE PUDDING.

Grate one half pound of cheese and add a dash of cayenne, and soda the size of a pea; add six ounces of grated bread, using crust and all; mix with pepper and salt to taste, melt two ounces of butter in one gill of boiling milk and pour over the mixture (cook in double boiler and stir until cheese is melted), then beat in the yolks of three eggs, beat whites of eggs stiff and add them to the mixture (after it is set off of the stove), then pour into a greased pudding dish and bake in moderately hot oven.

CHEESE STRAWS.

Sift one cupful of flour, one half teaspoonful of baking powder, a dash of cayenne pepper, and salt thoroughly. Then work in two tablespoonfuls butter, add three fourths of a cupful of grated cheese and mix to a soft dough with milk. Roll out lightly on a floured board, cut in strips the length of a pencil, also make some small rings. Bake in a hot oven until delicate brown. Put sticks through one or two of the rings. Nice to serve with salads, or for lunch boxes.

ESCALOPED POTATOES, WITH CHEESE.

Slice cold boiled potatoes and sprinkle with salt and pepper; prepare a good cream sauce; put a layer of sauce, then one of potato into a shallow bake dish, having the last layer of sauce; cut some thin strips of cheese about two and one half inches long, lay them on top of the potatoes, sprinkle with bread crumbs, put into a good oven till slightly browned and the cheese is somewhat melted.

CHEESE PATÉS, NO. 1.

Make a good short crust, roll it out very thin and line as many patty pans as will be required; fill them with stale bread crumbs, or dry rice. Cover with crust and bake in a quick oven. When cooked, remove the lid and take out the bread, or rice; fill up the case with cheese mixture; brush round the edge with egg and cover with the lid. Serve very hot.

Cheese Mixture.—Grate one half pound of good rich cheese, add a dash of cayenne pepper and a tiny speck of soda, mix with white sauce to the consistency of cream, stir over the fire until the mixture is thick, remove from stove, and add one well beaten yolk of egg. Fill the cases while hot and serve at once.

CHEESE PATÉS, NO. 2.

Cut rounds of bread two and one half inches thick and with a sharp knife or smaller cutter cut the center nearly through; spread all over with soft butter, put into a quick oven till a delicate brown, grate enough dry cheese to make one large cupful; season with salt, cayenne and a very little dry mustard; moisten with cream and stock till you have a smooth paste, adding a few drops of onion juice; fill the centers of the bread rounds; the cheese must not be too soft; put in a quick oven till cheese is melted, then draw to the edge of the oven; put a spoonful of beaten white of egg on top of each center, let color for a moment and serve.

CHEESE RELISH.

Fill a baking dish with alternate layers of grated cheese, in which you have mixed a tiny speck of soda, a dash of cayenne pepper, and bread crumbs, placing crumbs in bottom of dish. When filled, pour over it rich milk, or cream, in proportion of one half pint to each cupful of crumbs. Salt to taste and bake for twenty minutes in a reasonably hot oven.

CHEESE PUFF.

Butter liberally two slices of bread and place one in bottom of baking dish; grate one fourth pound of cheese and sprinkle half of it over the buttered bread with a little salt, a dash of cayenne pepper, and soda the size of a pea; then add another slice of buttered bread and the rest of the grated cheese; season as before; whip two eggs to a froth and beat into one pint of milk; pour it over the bread and cheese mixture and bake a delicate brown; serve hot.

CHEESE WAFERS.

Take a quarter of a pound each of flour, butter, and grated cheese; mix them thoroughly with one quarter of a saltspoonful of cayenne pepper. Mix with yolk of egg and water to a smooth stiff paste; roll this out to

the thickness of half an inch, then cut into pieces about
three inches long and one inch wide. Bake these until
they are lightly browned, and serve them as hot as
possible.

CHEESE CUSTARDS.

Six tablespoonfuls of grated cheese, two of butter,
four eggs, one cupful of milk with a teaspoonful of
corn starch stirred into it, salt and pepper to taste.
Beat the eggs very light and pour upon them the
heated milk (with a pinch of soda), having thickened
with the corn starch. While warm add butter, pepper, salt and cheese. Beat well and pour into greased
custard-cups. Bake in a quick oven about fifteen
minutes, or until high and brown. Serve at once, as a
separate course, with bread and butter, after soup, or
before serving dessert.

SALAD DRESSINGS, AND SALADS.

CREAM DRESSING.

To one pint of boiling cream, add two ounces of flour, stirred to a smooth paste with two ounces of butter; cook two minutes. Remove from sauce pan and add one ounce more of butter, stirring until cool and perfectly mixed; then season to taste with lemon juice, salt, pepper, and mustard (blending the mustard first in a little lemon juice). Add sliced olives; or, if preferred, use one tablespoonful of chopped parsley and one half teaspoonful of finely chopped onion; the olives are best with cabbage, and onion and parsley with mixed salads.

PLAIN DRESSING.

Beat one egg very light; add one tablespoonful of vinegar and cook in double boiler until thick; place one tablespoonful of butter in a bowl and pour the hot custard over it; beat until smooth, then add mustard and salt to taste—one half teaspoonful of mustard, and saltspoonful of salt is the usual proportion, —with half a teaspoonful of sugar to blend. Set away to cool. Just before using, add sufficient sweet cream to thin to the consistency of rich cream.

MAYONAISE DRESSING.

To the yolks of two eggs add a scant teaspoonful of mustard, equal quantity of salt, and a dash of cayenne pepper, stir, then add, very slowly almost drop by drop, one teacupful of olive oil. The mixture should be as thick as butter, then add one tablespoonful of lemon juice, if two thick, thin with sweet cream. For cabbage or potato salads it is well to add one half cup of sweet cream, while for tomato, aspic or plain, no cream should be used.

FRENCH DRESSING.

Mix one half teaspoonful of salt, with one half saltspoonful of pepper and two tablespoonfuls of lemon juice; then add slowly, stirring briskly, one half cupful of oil. Very nice for plain salads.

COOKED SALAD DRESSING.

Mix one tablespoonful of sugar, one teaspoonful of mustard, one teaspoonful of salt, a speck of cayenne and the yolk of one egg; add two tablespoonfuls of melted butter and one half cupful of milk. Stir over boiling water until it thickens. Take from the fire and add the beaten white of the egg and two tablespoonfuls of lemon juice.

AUNT SUSAN'S SALAD DRESSING.

Beat together one level teaspoonful of mustard, one heaping teaspoonful of sugar, one dessertspoonful of melted butter, one half teaspoonful of salt and the yolk of one egg; add one cupful of milk and cook in double boiler until it thickens; stirring all the while. When thick add lemon juice or vinegar to taste. This dressing can be kept any length of time by bottling, not necessary to seal.

SALAD CREAM.

Heat one half cupful of vinegar and one half cupful of sugar. When very hot add one half cupful of sour cream into which the yolks of two eggs have been beaten. Stir well, remove from the fire and then chill before using.

Very nice on cabbage salad.

SPRING SALAD.

In a salad bowl put a layer of fresh watercress, then a layer of thinly sliced cucumbers, then a layer of tomatoes with a teaspoonful of chopped chives. Repeat the process and put a border of watercress round the bowl. When ready to serve pour on a French dressing and toss until well mingled.

STUFFED TOMATO SALAD.

Select good sized, smooth, solid tomatoes, scald and skin quickly, slip into ice-water to chill, then carefully remove center without breaking under part; remove seed pulp with your finger, then fill with a chopped mixture of onion, cucumber, parsley, and cress; cover with mayonaise dressing and serve on platter garnished with lettuce leaves, or parsley. One should use judgment in regard to any mixture given-in receipt of this nature, and omit any article not pleasing to individual tastes, for instance some prefer to omit parsley, others do not like onion, etc.

PLAIN TOMATO SALAD.

Choose smooth round medium sized tomatoes, scald, and skin quickly. Set away to chill, serve on lettuce leaves with thick mayonaise dressing.

TOMATO ASPIC.

To one quart of strained tomato juice, add one bay leaf, one teaspoonful of chopped onion, and one teaspoonful of salt; let boil ten minutes, strain through fine sieve, or cheese cloth. Set back on stove and thicken with two or more tablespoonfuls of cornstarch, previously dissolved in one third cup of cold water; let boil until clear, turn into wet mould, and set away to chill. Serve on lettuce leaves with thick mayonaise dressing.

SUMMER SALAD.

Take two small heads of nice tender lettuce; tear, do not cut, add one pint of wax or string beans, that have been cooked till tender. Add one medium sized cucumber, sliced thin, and one young onion, two hard boiled eggs, sliced, add a dash of cayenne pepper, cover with mayonaise or French dressing.

ITALIAN SALAD.

Select two small heads of crisp tender lettuce, wash carefully; pare and slice one medium sized cucumber; cut fine one third cupful of parsley; wash one bunch of water cress; clean six crisp round radishes but do not pare, slice thin; slice very thin as much onion as suits your taste, mix all together and dress with oil, lemon juice, salt and cayenne pepper, mixed thoroughly until the lemon cuts the oil; this result is obtained more quickly if your oil is thoroughly chilled and is added slowly to the lemon juice and salt; add pepper last. This is a delicate and delicious summer salad.

STRING BEAN SALAD.

String, wash and break into inch lengths one quart of tender beans, boil in salted water until tender; drain thoroughly, then mix with one cupful of French dressing, and let stand until cold. Serve on lettuce leaves, and just before sending to the table add a little more dressing.

LIMA BEAN SALAD.

If fresh beans are used boil until tender in salted water; in winter use the California dried beans and soak over night, then boil gently till tender; drain, and when cold sprinkle with salt and pepper; add one tablespoonful of chopped parsley and a few drops of onion juice; pour over a French dressing, or, if you prefer, a mayonaise; arrange on crisp lettuce leaves, garnish with hard boiled eggs.

NUT AND CELERY SALAD.

To three cupfuls of finely cut celery, add one cupful of chopped English walnuts; dress liberally with mayonaise dressing, thinned with cream. Garnish with celery leaves and slices of lemon.

PLAIN CELERY SALAD.

Wash and finely cut the celery, and cover with mayonaise creamed dressing. Serve with slices of lemon.

POTATO AND CELERY SALAD.

Cut in dice one pint of cold, boiled, potatoes, add two cupfuls of finely cut celery. Pour over one half cupful of French dressing; let stand twenty minutes. Then cover with mayonaise and garnish with celery leaves and sliced lemon.

POTATO SALAD NO. 1.

Cut cold boiled potatoes into small dice, add one tablespoonful of onion juice, or tablespoonful of chopped onion (if onion flavor is liked). Sprinkle with celery seed and dress with oil, salt, cayenne, and lemon juice, the same as Italian salad.

POTATO SALAD NO. 2.

Arrange a parsley border and lay on slices of boiled potato, add a few drops of onion juice, or bits of finely chopped onion, or celery; then add finely chopped whites of hard boiled eggs; ornament the top with chopped parsley and yolks of boiled eggs, and dress liberally with French dressing. Chill before serving.

POTATO SALAD NO. 3.

Slice five or six cold boiled potatoes, one cucumber, a dozen olives, and three small onions, into a bowl; add half a teacupful of capers, a few chopped meats of English walnuts, and cover with mayonaise dressing.

BEET SALAD.

Boil small sized beets till tender in salted water; remove the skin, scoop out the center—leaving the sides one quarter of an inch thick; pour over them a French dressing to which has been added a few drops of onion juice; stand aside for an hour. Chop up four stalks of crisp celery and one cucumber; add one tablespoonful of chopped parsley, one half teaspoonful of onion juice and the chopped pieces of the beet taken from the centers; mix all together, drain the beets, and fill with the mixture; arrange on water cress, pour over it a French dressing.

CABBAGE SALAD.

Select a solid, white, head of cabbage, cut in half; then slice as finely as possible, with sharp knife or cabbage cutter the quanity desired; let stand in cold salted water for half an hour, drain thoroughly, and dress freely with cream dressing, to which has been added a dozen sliced olives, and a teaspoonful of chopped parsley.

SALAD OF GRAPE FRUIT AND WALNUTS.

Remove the pulp carefully from the grape fruit and add walnut meats in proportion of one half to the quanity of pulp; make a dressing of three tablespoonfuls of oil, with salt to taste, a dash of cayenne pepper, and one tablespoonful of lemon juice; pour this over the grape fruit and walnuts, and serve very cold.

A SWEET SALAD.

Slice bananas, and place in pudding, or salad dish, alternate layers of banana and strawberries, covering each layer liberally with sugar. Cover with whipped cream. Instead of strawberries, oranges may be used.

ORANGE SALAD.

Beat the yolks of four eggs until very thick and light colored, then beat into them, gradually, one cupful of sifted, powdered sugar and half a level teaspoonful of salt; beat until the sugar is dissolved. Next add the juice of two lemons and beat again. Peel and slice thin, six bananas. Peel four oranges, cutting close to the pulp, pick out the seeds, and slice oranges across in thin slices. Put into a deep glass dish a layer of bananas, then of the dressing, then of the orange, then again a layer of each in the same order with banana on the top, and pour the remainder of the dressing over it. Set on ice and serve very cold.

SALMAGUNDI.

Cut into neat strips three cold boiled potatoes, one carrot, one large beet, one half of a small cauliflower— all boiled and cold. Pile in attractive order on a flat dish; chop a cucumber pickle fine and strew over the pile, cover with raw tomatoes, pared and sliced; surround with crisp lettuce leaves as an outer bordering and pour mayonaise dressing over all. Pass a boat of dressing with the salad, also toasted crackers and cheese.

LETTUCE AND GRAPE FRUIT SALAD.

Tear a head of washed lettuce into pieces. Pare and divide into carpels one grape-fruit. With a pen-knife slit the white skin that envelops each carpel; take hold of the two ends, bend it back, and the fruit will fall out in little pieces, remove the seeds. Pour fruit and juice over the lettuce, and serve with a French dressing.

VEGETABLES.

CREAMED VEGETABLES.

Take equal quanities of carrots, turnips, asparagus, peas and cauliflowers. With a vegetable scoop cut the carrots and turnips into pieces a quarter of an inch square, or turn them into the shapes of olives, filberts, &c. Divide the cauliflowers and asparagus into small, neat pieces. Cook the vegetables separately in plenty of water; when tender drain and dry them; cover with white sauce and serve.

ESCALOPED ONIONS, CAULIFLOWER, OR ASPARAGUS.

Boil until tender, then put in baking dish and pour over sauce made of one tablespoonful of butter rubbed into one and one half tablespoonfuls of flour, pour over it one pint of hot milk, and cook until it is like a custard. Sprinkle thick with bread crumbs and bake one half hour. Cut the vegetables into small pieces before pouring over the sauce.

ASPARAGUS.

BAKED ASPARAGUS.

Place the asparagus with the root ends together in a baking dish; sprinkle in salt and black pepper; mix

two tablespoonfuls of flour smoothly with soft butter
to make a thin paste; spread it over the asparagus;
cover the dish with a plate; lay a weight on it; cook
it until the asparagus is very tender. It may be
served in the dish in which it is baked.

ASPARAGUS ON TOAST.

Cut away the hard ends; wash, then tie lightly
together in a large bunch with the heads all one way;
set in deep kettle with the heads up, fill with salted
water to within two inches of the top of the asparagus; cover and let boil until the stems are tender; the
steam will have cooked the tops. Have ready bread
toasted a delicate brown in the oven. Cut toast in
strips about two inches wide, lay it on hot shallow
dish or platter, butter liberally, drain the asparagus
and pile it on the toast; sprinkle liberally with butter,
pepper, and salt, and serve with cut lemon.

ASPARAGUS WITH WHITE SAUCE.

Make a good crust and line a baking dish, fill with
cooked asparagus, dress with the white sauce; cover
with top crust; and bake in hot oven.

ASPARAGUS PIE.

Make a good crust and line a baking dish filled
with cooked asparagus, dressed with the white sauce;
cover with top crust; and bake in hot oven.

ASPARAGUS PUDDING.

Beat together four eggs, a tablespoonful of butter,
pepper and salt. Add three tablespoonfuls of flour

mixed with one third teaspoonful of baking powder,
then a scant cupful of milk, and finally the boiled,
chopped tender tops of two bunches of asparagus.
Put into a well greased mould with a top, cook in a
pot of boiling water two hours; turn out and pour
over it a cupful of drawn butter.

BEANS.

CREAMED STRING BEANS.

Cut the ends and string them. Put them in a covered saucepan with water, and cook till tender, drain,
and remove any strings that may have adhered, then
place again in the pan, add one cupful of cold milk,
and salt to taste; thicken with flour mixed smoothly
with soft butter to the consistency of thick cream;
let them cook until the sauce is thoroughly done, add
a dash of pepper, and serve in hot covered dish.

WAX BEANS.

The yellow wax bean is very nice when young, prepare as you do any string bean, stew until tender,
letting liquor boil away and seasoning with salt, pepper, and butter.

BOSTON BAKED BEANS.

Small navy beans are the best. Carefully pick
over and wash one pint, soak over night in enough
water to cover; in the morning place in a kettle with

fresh water and boil for fifteen minutes; skim out of this water, and put into an earthen crock, add one large spoonful of molasses; one teaspoonful of mustard, salt to taste, and a large heaping tablespoonful of butter with water enough to cover; place a cover on the crock and set in the oven, cook them all day. They need to be watched at intervals of half an hour to see that the water is visible at the top of the beans; the last hour, if the oven is moderate, no more water should be added.

DRIED LIMA BEANS.

One cupful is sufficient for a family of five. Wash and put to soak over night. Steam in double boiler, with just water enough to float, until thoroughly tender. Salt to taste and add one tablespoonful of butter and a dash of pepper.

Dried beans can be freshened in an hour by soaking in hot water, and renewing the water as soon as it cools.

FRESH LIMA BEANS.

Boil until tender in just water enough to float, when nearly done, uncover and let water simmer away, add one cupful of sweet cream, and salt to taste just before serving. If you do not have cream, use milk, thickened with one teaspoonful of flour mixed with one tablespoonful of soft butter.

SUCCOTASH.

Take one cupful of cold cooked lima beans; add one half can of sweet corn, or equal quanity cut from cob; season to taste and add one teaspoonful of butter and one cupful of milk; cook until the corn is tender. Serve in hot, covered dish.

CORN.

ROASTED CORN.

Steam the ears until tender, then strip them, turn each ear in a flat plate in which there is a sufficiency of melted butter; then place them on a gridiron over a clean coal fire, and turn them until they are well toasted.

CUT CORN.

Steam the ears until tender, then strip them and cut the corn from the cob; add butter and seasoning to taste; place in hot covered dish; set in steamer until thoroughly heated through and serve very hot.

GREEN CORN—STEAMED.

Select nice full ears; and place in steamer with the husks on. Steam an hour or more until tender then strip the ears; cutting off both ends; heap the corn on a hot shallow dish and set in the oven a minute or two to dry.

CORN FRITTERS.

In the summer when fresh corn can be had, grate the corn from the cob and mix in proportion of one cupful of grated corn to three well beaten eggs; salt to taste and fry in hot butter by spoonfuls; serve hot. They are much more delicate and delicious than where flour and milk are used. The corn supplies both the milk and flour in its own substance. Grated, or very tender, canned corn can be used in the same way in the winter season.

BAKED CORN.

Chop as fine as possible the contents of one can of corn add a heaping tablespoonful of butter; season to taste; add one pint of milk put in baking dish; place in oven and bake until a nice brown.

CORN PUDDING.

Cut enough uncooked corn from the cob to fill a pint measure; place in covered sauce pan with a pint of cold milk; let cook until tender; then add two table-spoonfuls of flour smoothly mixed with cold milk. Stir until the mixture thickens; add two tablespoonfuls of butter; set it off to cool.

Beat the yolks of four eggs in a large bowl; beat whites separately to a stiff froth; then mix well with the yolks, add to the warm corn and milk mixture, put into a hot buttered baking dish and brown in quick oven.

CORN ON TOAST.

Take pieces of bread four inches square and fry a delicate brown in butter; then heap on the bread a large teablespoonful of stewed or canned corn and heat through thoroughly; serve very hot.

CORN PATÊS.

Chop finely half a can of corn; stir in bread crumbs until stiff; season with salt and pepper; fill patê shells two thirds full and lay piece of butter size of hickory nut on top of each filling; then pour over each one a tablespoonful of cream; place in oven and bake till delicate brown; serve hot. Very much like oysters.

If creamy dressing is preferred, omit the bread crumbs, and thicken the cream with a little flour and butter before pouring over the corn, use a little more cream to each shell.

CABBAGE.

TO BOIL CABBAGE.

Wash in cold water, and pick over very carefully. Put whole in a covered boiler, with the stem end down, sprinkle well with salt, pour over it a cupful of cold water, boil until it is very tender, then uncover it for the water to boil away; set it on the back of range to dry, take off the coarse outer leaves, serve it in a hot, deep, dish. Cut the cabbage into halves or quarters and lay butter on each piece.

CABBAGE IN WHITE SAUCE.

Cut a head of white cabbage in pieces two or three inches large, put them into a covered saucepan with salt, one cupful of cold water, and flour mixed to a smooth thin paste with soft butter; boil until the cabbage is very tender.

CABBAGE IN MILK.

Chop coarsely one-fourth large or one-half small head of cabbage; put over in saucepan with enough salted water to float; let cook until nearly done, then drain; add one quart of rich milk and cook until tender; add salt, pepper, and butter to taste.

HOT SLAW.

Chop one half large, or one small head of cabbage; put over in saucepan with salted water; cook till tender, but not soft; drain, add one-half cupful of vinegar, salt and pepper to taste, with one tablespoonful of butter.

BAKED CABBAGE.

Boil a firm, white, head of cabbage until tender, drain, and set aside until cold. Then chop fine; add two well beaten eggs; one ounce of butter; salt, and pepper, with three tablespoonfuls of cream; bake in moderate oven.

EGG PLANT.

ESCALOPED EGG PLANT.

Steam a whole egg plant until it is soft throughout; cut it in half, lengthwise; put each half into a vegetable dish; cut it in squares; sprinkle them with salt and moisten with Worcestershire Sauce; spread butter over them; dredge with powdered crackers; strew with pieces of butter and brown in a quick oven.

BAKED EGG PLANT.

Peel and cut in pieces enough egg plant to fill a quart bowl; steam until it can be mashed smooth; stir in two tablespoonfuls of butter, one tablespoonful of salt, and one half teaspoonful of black pepper; put it into a baking dish; smooth it over, dredge it with powdered cracker; strew it with pieces of butter; and brown it in a quick oven.

FRIED EGG PLANT.

Cut it crosswise into thin slices; fry them immediately in boiling cocoanut butter or vegetable oil; sprinkle both sides with salt and black pepper; cover the frying pan with a tin cover; set it on the back of range to steam until the egg plant is very tender; serve on a hot shallow dish.

EGG PLANT IN EGG AND CRACKER.

Cut it in thin slices across; fry it immediately in hot cocoanut butter or vegetable oil; lay the slices on a cold dish; sprinkle both sides with salt and black pepper; pour beaten egg over to moisten both sides; turn each slice in powered cracker; fry them a second time in the boiling fat; lay them on a hot dish; serve them brown and crisp.

EGG PLANT BALLS.

Prepare as for baked egg plant; roll a tablespoonful into round balls in the palms of the hands, flatten them, pour beaten egg over them to moisten both sides, turn each in a plate of powdered crackers, fry them brown in boiling fat, and serve them on a hot shallow dish.

PEAS.

GREEN PEAS.

Do not wash peas, as it spoils their flavor and makes them less nutritious. Peas should not be shelled until immediately before using.

TO BOIL PEAS.

Put them into a covered saucepan, with cold water enough to float them; boil them until the peas are tender; then uncover them for the water to boil away; set them at the back of range to dry; serve them in a hot, covered, vegetable dish, with a tablespoonful of butter laid on them; or, if liked, one cupful of cream may be added just before removing from saucepan.

PEAS IN WHITE SAUCE.

Put the peas into a saucepan, with one cupful of cold water, and one teaspoonful of flour, mixed smoothly with soft butter to make a thin paste. Cover the saucepan, and boil the peas until they are very tender; add one-half cupful of cream and serve in a hot, covered dish.

PATÊS WITH PEAS.

Make little shells of puff paste and dress with peas stewed tender, to which has been added cream, thickened slightly with flour and butter.

PASTRY WITH PEAS.

Make little shells of pie crust and fill with young peas cooked tender and seasoned with pepper, salt, and butter; the peas should be carefully drained before filling the shells.

POTATOES.

BOILED POTATOES.

Boiled potatoes are more nutritious when boiled in the skin. They should be placed in a kettle with a sufficient amount of cold water to cover them, salted to taste, cooked in an uncovered kettle, and the water permitted to boil away; then let kettle remain on the back of range where they will keep hot, until the potatoes are dry and mealy. Peel before serving.

NEW POTATOES.

Small new potatoes with white skins need not be peeled, but should be buttered liberally and served in a hot dish.

MASHED POTATOES.

Boil until tender and place in colander, have ready a large bowl with tablespoonful of butter and half a cupful of cream; mash through the colander into a bowl, then whip potatoes and seasoning thoroughly with a fork, as a spoon destroys the delicacy; place in dish and set uncovered over steam to heat thoroughly. Serve quickly,

POTATO CROQUETTES.

To one pint of hot mashed potatoes add one tablespoonful of butter, one half saltspoonful of pepper, one half teaspoonful of salt, one dash of cayenne, one half teaspoonful celery salt, and a few drops of onion juice. Beat until very light. When slightly cooled, mix in yolk of one egg; add one teaspoonful of chopped parsley. Shape into croquettes, roll in fine bread crumbs, then in a mixture of egg and milk, roll again in bread crumbs, let stand about fifteen minutes in a cold place, then fry by plunging in very hot fat for a moment. Do not fry more than three at a time, in order not to chill the fat. Drain carefully.

POTATO PATÊS.

Take a tablespoonful of warm mashed potato in the palm of your hand, shaping it like a ball; then with a teaspoon take out a good part of the center. Fill this potato patê shell with minced onion and celery cooked tender in butter, and add a grating of cheese; season to taste, then cover it over with potato;

dip into melted butter and egg; place in a shallow baking pan and place in a hot oven, let come to a nice brown; serve on platter garnished with parsley.

SARATOGA CHIPS.

Select medium sized potatoes, pare, wash, and slice them very thin; dry with a napkin. Have kettle of cocoa butter, or oil, heated to right temperature (see "Important Notes") and sprinkle potatoes in kettle; do not crowd; when a delicate brown, skim out, and place in sieve in a warm place to drain; sprinkle lightly with salt.

PRINCESS POTATOES.

Boil and mash the desired quantity; while the potatoes are still warm spread them half an inch thick on a plate and set away to cool. When ready to use them, cut the potato into strips an inch wide and two inches long; dip the strips into melted butter, and then into well beaten egg, finally placing them in a baking pan and browning them in a hot oven.

WACHTMEISTER POTATOES.

Select potatoes of medium size and perfect shape; scour the skins, and steam until tender, then place in oven until skin is slightly toughened; remove from oven and open at one end, carefully removing contents, do not break the skins. Have ready a bowl of whipped cream; mash the potatoes and mix freely with whipped cream. Stuff back in potato skins and set in shallow dish, open ends up; place back in oven and let them get thoroughly hot, then serve. One who has been a strict vegetarian for years finds salt a poison; and it is omitted intentionally in the "Wachtmeister" receipt. It can of course be added to potato in mixing for those who desire it.

POTATOES IN WHITE SAUCE.

Peel and quarter potatoes, put them into saucepan (with salt, if desired) add flour and butter, mixed to a smooth paste, in the proportion of one tablespoonful of flour to two of soft butter, a teaspoonful of chopped parsley and just water enough to float potatoes; cover the saucepan and cook until potatoes are very tender.

LYONNAISE POTATOES.

To one tablespoonful of finely chopped onion, add seasoning to taste; place in frying pan with two tablespoonfuls of butter and let fry a light brown, being careful not to burn. Have ready one quart of cold boiled potato cut in small dice, add and turn delicately with fork until potatoes have absorbed the butter; just before removing from fire add one tablespoonful of chopped parsley. Serve very hot.

ESCALOPED POTATOES.

Pare, wash and slice enough potatoes to nearly fill a baking dish; season to taste, fill the dish with cold milk and add one large tablespoonful of butter distributed over the top, bake in moderate oven, keeping dish covered until potatoes are nearly done. Then remove cover and brown.

FRENCH FRIED POTATOES.

Peel and cut in strips medium or small potatoes, wash, then dry with a clean towel. Have ready a kettle of cocoa butter thoroughly hot, drop in potatoes and cook until a delicate brown; if salt is used sprinkle slightly when taken from the fat, let drain in wire dish in the oven one minute, then serve in hot dish.

FRIED POTATOES.

A nice way to fry potatoes is to dip them in egg and then in bread crumbs; then fry until brown.

POTATO SCONES.

Boil potatoes in salted water; three good-sized potatoes making a sufficient supply for moderate family; drain and mash; mix with just enough flour to enable you to roll out the mixture, cut with biscuit cutter and bake on an ungreased griddle, turning frequently. The scones should have the thickness and consistency of wheat pancakes.

POTATO PEARS.

Cook five potatoes and rub through a strainer. While hot add two tablespoonfuls of butter, one half teaspoonful of salt, one fourth teaspoonful of celery salt, one fourth teaspoonful of pepper, a few grains of cayenne, and one teaspoonful of chopped parsley. Beat thoroughly and add yolk of one egg. Shape in the form of pears. Beat one egg, slightly diluting with two tablespoonfuls of milk. Roll the pears in the egg, then in crumbs, and fry in deep fat; dry on brown

paper. Insert a clove at the blossom and stem of each
pear. Garnish with parsley.

POTATO PANCAKES.

Grate six large potatoes; drain, and add pint of
cream or milk, two well beaten eggs, one tablespoonful of flour, and beat well. Melt one teaspoonful of
butter in frying pan, pour in a thin layer of batter; as
it cooks loosen it from the pan, when a delicate brown,
turn, and brown. Serve hot.

SWEET POTATOES.

BAKED SWEET POTATOES.

Wash carefully, cutting out any bruised spots;
place in steamer. When they are tender put them
in a quick oven to roast to a delicate crust.

ESCALOPED SWEET POTATOES.

Pare medium sized potatoes; cut into halves or
into three slices, according to size; place a layer in a
baking pan, add bits of butter, pepper, and a generous
sprinkling of sugar; then add another layer of potatoes and seasoning. When all have been used, add
enough boiling water to show through them, but not
quite enough to cover them. Cover the pan and bake
one hour in a moderate oven; then remove cover and
bake one half hour longer until the potatoes are nicely
browned on top. Serve in the dish in which they are
baked.

SWEET POTATO CURRY.

Pare potatoes and cut into dice, about an inch in size; sprinkle with curry powder and brown in two tablespoonfuls of butter. When they are half cooked salt, pepper and cover with soup stock; boil until tender.

SWEET POTATO CROQUETTES.

Boil, peel, and mash six large sweet potatoes; season with salt, a tablespoonful of butter, one of sugar and a little pepper. When cold, mold into croquettes, dip into beaten egg, then into finely rolled bread crumbs, and fry brown in hot fat.

GLACED SWEET POTATOES.

Cut cold boiled, or steamed potatoes, into slices about an inch thick and season to taste. For one pint of potatoes, melt one fourth cupful of butter and add one tablespoonful of sugar. Dip the slices into this liquid and lay them on a large pan. Cook for twelve minutes in a very hot oven, or until they become a rich glossy brown. Serve hot.

FRIED SWEET POTATOES.

Peel and slice sweet potatoes about one fourth inch thick; fry in deep fat for about ten minutes, drain on a brown paper in warm oven for a few minutes, sprinkle with salt; serve hot.

BROWNED SWEET POTATO.

After potatoes are steamed until tender, peel and

cut them in lengthwise strips; brown in hot cocoanut butter or vegetable oil.

WARMED UP SWEET POTATOES.

Any left over cold steamed potatoes can be made into a relish by peeling, slicing and frying a delicate brown in butter.

ONIONS.

Steam old onions; stew young onions.

TO STEAM ONIONS.

Put them whole into a baking dish, covered with a plate; set it in a hot oven to steam for three or more hours; take off the coarse outer skin and serve the onions in a hot, covered, vegetable dish, with butter, salt, and black pepper.

STEWED ONIONS.

Peel young onions and put them into a covered saucepan; add salt, one cupful of cold water, flour mixed smoothly with soft butter to make a thin paste, and one tablespoonful of chopped parsley; stew them until they are thoroughly tender; serve them in a hot covered dish.

YOUNG ONIONS IN WHITE SAUCE.

Select the young onions with green tops, cutting off the coarse part of the top; boil until tender; drain; place in vegetable dish and sprinkle with pepper and

salt; add teaspoonful of butter; have ready one pint
of milk, scalded and thickened with heaping teaspoonful of flour blended with melted butter, boiled sufficiently to thoroughly cook flour. Pour over the onions
and serve.

BAKED ONIONS.

Bermuda, or large Spanish, onions are the best for
baking. although the ordinary white onion will do;
set them without peeling in a large pan of salted
water, to which add one cupful of milk; boil until
tender; drain and remove skins, put in baking pan;
sprinkle with salt and pepper; add a very little of the
water they were boiled in, and set in oven to brown.
Pour melted butter over them and serve.

FRIED ONIONS.

Peel large onions; slice them very thin in rounds;
sprinkle them with salt and red pepper; brown them
in boiling cocoa butter, or vegetable oil; cover the
frying pan with a tin cover; set it on the range to
steam until the onions are very tender; serve them
heaped on a hot, shallow dish; garnish them thickly
with sprigs of fresh parsley to neutralize the odor
after they are eaten.

ONIONS IN MILK.

Peel small white onions; nearly fill a quart bottle;
put in two tablespoonfuls of soft butter mixed to a
paste with a tablespoonful of flour, one teaspoonful
of salt, and one half teaspoonful of white pepper; pour

in a pint of cold milk; cork the bottle; set it in a saucepan of cold water over the fire to boil an hour or more; serve it turned into a hot covered dish.

Wash the leaves in cold water; shake out each leaf, and heap them on a colander to drain.

SPINACH.

TO BOIL SPINACH.

Put the leaves into a kettle to boil twenty minutes; then uncover the saucepan so as to boil the juice nearly away; turn the spinach into a colander; drain them into a hot vegetable dish, in which is butter, salt, and black pepper; turn it into the butter and salt; serve it with poached eggs on the top.

CHOPPED SPINACH WITH EGGS.

After spinach is boiled and dried, chop it in the saucepan very fine with a knife; set it over the fire again to dry; stir in butter, salt, and black pepper; break in two or more eggs; stir them with the spinach and let them cook until it looks quite dry; serve it in a hot vegetable dish.

SPINACH SOUFFLE.

Boil and dry spinach; chop it very fine in the saucepan and let it dry; stir in two tablespoonfuls of butter, one teaspoonful of salt, and one half teaspoonful of black pepper; let the butter be absorbed. Beat the yolks of two eggs in a large bowl, beat the whites to a stiff froth, mix them well into the yolks, stir in the hot seasoned spinach with a fork, and bake it in a hot buttered dish in a quick oven until the top is well browned.

TOMATOES.

TOMATO ON TOAST.

Use stale bread, cut in reasonably thick slices; dip in sweet milk, then in beaten egg, seasoned with salt and pepper; fry in butter till a nice brown. Have ready a quart of tomatoes that have stewed gently until reduced one fourth; season to taste; add one table-spoonful of butter and pour over fried toast. Just before serving place a poached egg on each slice.

STUFFED BAKED TOMATOES.

Select good-sized, smooth, solid fruit; wash, do not pare; cut out the hard center and remove seed pulp with finger. Fill in with mixture made of two cupfuls of bread crumbs, wet with one tablespoonful of melted butter; add two tablespoonfuls of chopped onion, one cupful of chopped celery, season to taste; heap the filling in tomatoes and put a piece of butter on top; place in earthen pie dish to bake. They should be in the oven until well browned on top; serve on squares of bread that have been fried a nice brown, in butter.

FRIED TOMATOES.

Wash and slice the tomatoes, without paring; sprinkle with seasoning, dip in flour, cook in frying pan with butter, a liberal supply of grease is required. Cover for a few minutes, so the tomatoes may steam through, and not brown too quickly, as they need to be well cooked; turn and brown on both sides. Serve on toast.

FRICASSEED TOMATOES.

Select large smooth tomatoes; cut them in half, do not peel. Take a broad agate, or enameled pan and melt in it two ounces of butter; cover the pan with the halved tomatoes that have been sprinkled with salt, and pepper, and dipped in meal; whole wheat flour is best. Put cover on pan and let cook until tomatoes are cooked through, but not broken. The fire should be moderate, and it is well to lift the tomatoes occasionally so they will not burn or stick to pan. When cooked, pour in one half cupful sweet cream, let come to a scald, and serve.

ESCALOPED TOMATOES.

Fill baking dish with alternate layers of bread crumbs and cold stewed tomatoes, well seasoned, finishing with bread crumbs on top, and break in bits over the top one heaping tablespoonful of butter, and bake until brown.

TOMATO AND RICE FRITTERS.

Add one teacupful of cold stewed tomatoes to two

cupfuls of cold boiled rice; season to taste; bind with
one egg well whipped; mould into smooth little shapes,
and fry in butter.

DEVILLED TOMATOES.

Take two or three large firm tomatoes, not over
ripe, cut them in slices half an inch thick and lay on a
seive. Make a dressing of one tablespoonful of butter
and one of vinegar rubbed smooth with the yolk of
one hard boiled egg; add a very little sugar, salt,
mustard and cayenne pepper; beat until smooth and
heat to a boil. Take from the fire and pour upon a
well beaten egg whipping to a smooth cream. Put the
vessel containing this dressing in hot water while the
tomatoes are being broiled over a clear fire. Put the
tomatoes on a hot dish and pour the dressing over
them.

BREAD STUFFS.

HOME MADE YEAST.

Wash, pare, and soak one large potato. Steep one tablespoonful of hops (loose) in one pint of boiling water; mix one heaping tablespoonful of flour, one teaspoonful of sugar, one teaspoonful of salt, one teaspoonful of ginger; grate the potato into the flour mixture; let the hot water boil briskly for one minute, strain it over the flour and potato mixture, and mix thoroughly; if it does not thicken like starch, place it over the fire for a few minutes, stirring briskly. If too thick, add boiling water till thin as cream. When lukewarm or at 70 degrees, add one half cake of yeast. Raise in a warm place till frothy, beat it down every half hour. Bottle and keep in a cool place.

THREE HOUR BREAD.

Pour one cupful of boiling water over two tablespoonfuls of flour and beat well; when this becomes lukewarm add two teaspoonfuls of sugar and one yeast cake that has been dissolved in one half cupful of lukewarm water. Beat thoroughly, add flour enough to make a thick batter, beat until light and set in a warm place, about 90 degrees F. Keep covered and let rise until light and frothy, with this proportion

of yeast it should rise in thirty minutes. When light
add one cupful of scalded milk, cooled to lukewarm,
and flour enough to make a stiff dough; stir in
the flour with a spoon, beating it thoroughly;
when the dough begins to stiffen, cut in the flour
with a bread knife; add flour until the dough slips
easily from the board, and does not stick to the
hands. Then knead the dough on a slightly floured
board until smooth, elastic, and full of air bub-
bles. Knead it firmly, but lightly, using only the
wrist movements, put back in bowl, cover, and let rise
in warm place until it doubles in bulk; shape into
loaves, or biscuit; brush lightly with melted butter,
and place in warm buttered pan. Let rise, closely
covered, until loaves have doubled in bulk. Bake in
an oven hot enough to brown one teaspoonful of flour
placed on a piece of paper, in five minutes. If biscuit
are to be baked, the oven should be hot enough to
brown flour in two minutes. Let the bread bake from
forty-five minutes to one hour. The first quarter of
the time the bread should rise, but not form a crust;
the second quarter the crust should form; the third
the crust should become golden brown; the fourth
should complete the baking. Place the loaf to cool
uncovered, and in such a position that the air can
circulate freely around it, bottom and all.

WHOLE WHEAT BREAD.

Make a sponge of one half cupful lukewarm water,
one half yeast cake dissolved in one fourth cupful luke-

warm water, and one cupful of white flour; cover; and set in warm place,—about 90 degrees F.—until light and foamy; add one half cupful scalded milk, cooled to lukewarm, one half teaspoonful of salt and whole wheat flour to make a stiff dough; knead thoroughly, put into warm place, let rise until it doubles in bulk; mould into a loaf, put into a warm buttered pan, and keep closely covered in warm place until it rises sufficiently to double in size; put into a hot oven; at the end of fifteen minutes lower the temperature of oven and bake at least forty-five minutes longer. This makes one loaf.

ENGLISH UNFERMENTED GRIDDLE BREAD.

This bread is usually made from whole wheat flour. It is cooked on a griddle, hence its name "Griddle Bread." The griddle should be made thoroughly hot before placing the dough on it, and sprinkled with a little fine white flour. Measure the meal, and for every two level measures of meal allow one measure of boiling water; have the meal in a mixing bowl, and use a wooden spoon for stirring. Make a hole in the center of the meal and pour the boiling water into it, stirring all the time till it forms a mass or lump. No kneading is required. Sprinkle the paste-board with fine white flour and turn the mass onto it. Roll out into cakes, making the cake about half an inch thick. The edge should not be ragged, but dredged with fine flour and pressed with the knuckles to an even thickness. Dredge fine flour on each piece, rub it well in with the

fingers, then turn it on the other side with the knife
and do the same, so that the surface has a fine smooth
appearance. As each piece is prepared, place it on
the hot griddle plate. Two or three minutes is sufficient time to prepare the bread from the moment the
water boils. The time for the cooking necessarily
varies according to the heat of the fire, which should
be kept at an even temperature; twenty to thirty
minutes will be found the average.

TEA ROLLS.

Make a sponge of one cupful of lukewarm water,
one cake of yeast, one fourth cupful sugar, and flour
enough to make a soft dough. When sufficiently
raised add a little over a cupful of softened
butter, and three fourths of a cupful of luke warm
milk and enough flour to keep it a sponge. Beat
well and let rise; then add beaten white of one egg
and enough flour to knead. Knead thoroughly and let
it rise again; work down; place in a buttered bowl;
let it rise again, turn onto a board, roll, and cut.
Shape to suit fancy, in finger rolls, bread sticks, or
cleft rolls; place in pans and let rise; bake in hot oven.
For Cinnamon Rolls, make as above only roll out one
fourth inch in thickness and spread with softened
butter, sugar, cinnamon, and currants. All bread
stuffs brown better if brushed over with melted butter.

WHOLE WHEAT MUFFINS.

Take one and one half cupfuls of whole wheat
flour, one cupful of common flour, two teaspoonfuls of

baking powder, mix, and sift together; beat up one
egg and add one cupful of milk; add one tablespoonful of melted butter and stir into the dry mixture;
bake in gem pans in a hot oven for about twenty
minutes.

CORN MUFFINS.

Mix thoroughly one cupful of white flour, one half
cupful of fine yellow corn meal, one eighth cupful of
sugar, two tablespoonfuls of baking powder; then beat
one egg and stir in one cupful of sweet milk; stir into
dry mixture; then add one tablespoonful of melted
butter; beat well, and bake in muffin tins.

GRAHAM OR RYE GEMS.

To one and one half cupfuls of graham, or rye flour,
measured after sifting, add one eighth cupful of sugar,
two teaspoonfuls of baking powder, one half cupful
of white flour and mix thoroughly; then add one cupful of sweet milk and two tablespoonfuls of melted
butter, and stir quickly. Put in hot gem pans, bake for
twenty-five minutes in hot oven.

BAKING POWDER BISCUIT.

To one pint of sifted flour add two teaspoonfuls of
baking powder; sift together twice; then rub in one
tablespoonful of shortening until fine, like meal. Mix
in gradually enough milk to make a soft dough, cutting it in with bread knife; when stiff enough to be
handled it should look spongy in the cuts, and seem
full of air; turn it out on a well floured board, toss

with knife until well floured, pat with rolling pin, and when dough is about half an inch thick, cut it into rounds and bake at once in hot oven.

PUFFS.

Sift one teaspoonful of baking powder into two cupfuls of flour; with one half teaspoonful of salt; add two cupfuls of milk and two eggs, beat the yolks and the whites of the eggs separately. Bake in gem pans in quick oven.

POP-OVERS.

With one cupful of flour, mix one saltspoonful of salt; add slowly one cupful of milk; when a smooth paste is formed add one cupful more of milk and one egg beaten thoroughly; beat well; cook in hot buttered gem pans or earthen cups in a quick oven for half an hour, or until the puffs are brown and well popped over. The more the milk and flour are beaten the lighter the puffs will be.

WAFFLES.

Sift together one pint of flour, one teaspoonful of baking powder, one teaspoonful of salt; add one and one fourth cupfuls of milk to smooth the batter; then add the well beaten yolks of three eggs; beat well; then whip in one tablespoonful of melted butter; and add the stiffly beaten whites of the eggs, cutting and folding these in. Have waffle-iron hot and well greased; butter as soon as taken from the iron. Sugar can be added at the same time, if relished.

BOSTON BROWN BREAD.

Take one pint each of whole wheat flour and Indian meal, one cupful of molasses, three fourths cupful of sour milk, and one half teaspoonful of soda, one and one half pints of cold water, mix; put in steamer on stove over cold water, which is afterwards brought to the boiling point and kept constantly boiling until bread is done; steam for four hours, and brown in the oven. Just before putting in the steamer add one cupful of seeded raisins.

BANNOCKS.

Two teacupfuls of oatmeal, or barley meal, sifted with two teaspoonfuls of baking powder; add two beaten eggs one tablespoonful of sugar and one pint of milk with a little salt, sifting in the meal. Mix and bake on a griddle.

GRIDDLE CAKES.

To one cupful of flour, add one saltspoonful of salt, one tablespoonful of baking powder; sift thoroughly; add milk enough to make a batter like a thick cream; then whip in one teaspoonful of melted butter. One egg may be well beaten and added, though it is not necessary.

This receipt can be varied by using graham, corn, or whole wheat flour, in proportions of two thirds graham or wheat to one third white flour. Corn should only be one third corn to two thirds white flour.

HOMINY GRIDDLE CAKES.

To one cupful of sweet milk, add one cupful of warm, fine, boiled hominy; add one half teaspoonful of salt, two eggs,—whites and yolks beaten separately, —one teaspoonful of melted butter. In mixing add well beaten whites of eggs last. Use flour enough to make thin batter. Can be cooked either as griddle cakes or waffles.

RAISED GRAHAM GRIDDLE CAKES.

One cupful of graham meal, one cupful of flour, one half yeast cake dissolved in one quarter of a cupful of lukewarm water, mix with this one pint of milk scalded and cooled, and let it rise over night. In the morning add one tablespoonful of molasses, and one saltspoonful of soda. If the batter is too thick add a little warm water.

INDIAN MEAL GRIDDLE CAKES.

One pint of Indian meal, one teaspoonful of sugar, one teaspoonful of butter, add gradually to this sufficient boiling milk to wet the meal; when cool add two well beaten eggs, and sufficient cold milk to make a thin batter.

BREAD GRIDDLE CAKES.

One pint of stale bread crumbs; pour over them one pint of hot milk; add one tablespoonful of butter; when the crumbs are soft rub through a strainer and add the beaten yolks of two eggs, one cupful of flour, and two teaspoonfuls of baking powder. If the batter is not thin enough add a little cold milk.

RICE GRIDDLE CAKES.

Take one cupful of sweet milk, one cupful of warm boiled rice, the yolks of two eggs beaten until light, one tablespoonful of melted butter, and flour enough to make a thin batter; stir in lastly the whites of the eggs beaten stiff and dry. Bake on a hot griddle.

SOUR MILK GRIDDLE CAKES.

Sift one half teaspoonful of salt and one teaspoonful of soda into one pint of flour; add one scant pint of sour milk or cream, the beaten yolks of two eggs, and lastly the whites beaten very stiff. Bake on a hot, well greased griddle.

BREAKFAST FOODS.

WHOLE WHEAT.

Sift one cupful of whole wheat meal into one pint of boiling water; add salt to taste. Cook in double boiler and steam from one to two hours, until meal is thoroughly cooked. Very nice when cold fried in delicate slices and served with maple syrup.

Graham, rye, oat meal, or corn meal can be cooked in same way, only they require longer cooking. Corn requires the most time. Corn and oat meals need a larger quantity of water.

SANDWICHES.

CHEESE AND EGG SANDWICHES.

Beat two eggs in a bowl for two minutes, add two tablespoonfuls of milk, one eighth tablespoonful of salt, a sprinkle of white pepper; melt one half tablespoonful of butter in a small frying pan, pour in the eggs, stir until they begin to thicken, then sprinkle over one tablespoonful of freshly grated bread crumbs and two tablespoonfuls of cheese, stir for a few minutes longer, remove and put one tablespoonful of this preparation between two thin slices of bread.

EGG SANDWICH.

Break two eggs in a small bowl and beat until they foam; add a sprinkle of salt. Place a small frying pan over the fire with one tablespoonful of butter; as soon as butter is melted pour in the eggs, stir until they thicken, then remove. Butter four thin slices of bread, cover two with the eggs; lay over the remaining two slices; trim them neatly and cut them slantingly in half.

NUT-SANDWICHES. No. 1.

Mix equal parts of grated Swiss cheese and chopped English walnut meat. Season with salt and cayenne. Spread between thin slices of bread slightly buttered, and cut in fancy shapes.

NUT SANDWICHES. No. 2.

Shell one half pint of peanuts and roll them fine
with the rolling pin. Stir the yolk of one hard boiled
egg to a cream with one half tablespoonful of butter,
add one teaspoonful of French mixed mustard, one
quarter teaspoonful of salt, one tablespoonful of lemon
juice, one half tablespoonful of unsweetened con-
densed milk, one half cupful of finely chopped red
apple, the finely chopped white of an egg, and the
nuts. Put one tablespoonful of this mixture between
two thin slices of bread; trim them evenly all around,
and cut them slantingly into two pieces.

PLAIN CHEESE SANDWICH.

Butter the bread; lay thin slices of cream cheese
to cover, add a lettuce leaf, and cover with another
piece of buttered bread.

COTTAGE CHEESE SANDWICH.

Use crisp, square crackers, wet the cottage cheese
with sweet cream, season to taste, and spread on
crackers.

OLIVE AND CAPER SANDWICHES.

Chop olives very fine, add one third as much of
finely chopped capers; mix thoroughly with a little
soft butter; season with celery salt, cayenne, a very
few drops of lemon juice, and a little of the grated
lemon peel. Spread on thin squares of buttered graham bread.

CHEESE AND MUSTARD SANDWICH.

Grate one fourth pound of cheese and mix one half teaspoonful of salt and mustard, with a dash of cayenne pepper; melt one tablespoonful of butter and blend with seasoning; then stir thoroughly into the cheese; if liked, a teaspoonful of lemon juice may be added. Spread on thin slices of whole wheat, or white, bread.

BOILED EGG SANDWICHES.

Chop the whites of hard boiled eggs very fine; blend the yolks with a little cream or melted butter, season to taste, and spread on buttered white bread.

TOMATO SANDWICH.

Cut thin slices of brown bread; spread with French mustard; then a layer of cream cheese; sprinkle lightly with salt; peel and slice some small, solid, ripe tomatoes. Cover the prepared bread with the slices; form into sandwiches and cut in broad strips. Serve with water cress.

TOMATO AND EGG SANDWICH.

Chop the whites of four hard boiled eggs very fine. Mash the yolks and blend with a little thick cream, some tomato pulp, salt, pepper, and a tiny pinch of sugar. Spread on thin slices of brown, buttered, bread.

CHOCOLATE SANDWICH.

Melt one ounce of grated chocolate; whip in a little hot cream; add one half teaspoonful of vanilla flavoring, a little confectioner's sugar, and the yolk of one egg. Stir until it begins to thicken, then whip in the whites of the egg beaten to a stiff froth.

Spread on thin slices of sponge cake, or white bread and butter.

MUSHROOM SANDWICHES.

Stew a few large mushrooms in one ounce of butter; cover closely and cook slowly so that they shall not burn; mash them with pepper, salt, and a dash of nutmeg; cut thin slices of whole wheat bread, butter and spread with the mushroom paste. Cut into finger sandwiches.

PINEAPPLE SANDWICH.

Cut small sweet sponge buns in slices; spread them with grated pineapple; sift with fine sugar; press two slices together and spread soft icing on top and sides.

ITALIAN SANDWICHES.

Make a mixture of chopped olives, grated cheese and chopped English walnuts in the proportion of two fifths each of cheese and olives to one fifth of nuts; then make a dressing of five tablespoonfuls of malt vinegar (or six, if ordinary vinegar is used) bring to a scald and stir into the well beaten yolks of five eggs; set the egg mixture back on the stove and stir constantly until it becomes as thick as cream; then remove from the stove and beat in one tablespoonful of butter, whipping until the butter is dissolved and thoroughly blended. Season to taste with salt, pepper and mustard; if liked add a dash of cayenne. Stir in the chopped olives, nuts, and cheese. Spread between crisp square crackers, or thin slices of whole wheat bread.

FRUIT SANDWICHES.

Slice whole wheat or graham bread very thin, butter, then spread with a layer of chopped raisins, or candied cherries wet with orange juice.

GRAHAM SANDWICHES.

Chop olives; add a little chopped parsley and a little finely chopped celery; mix with mayonnaise dressing to which has been added a few drops of onion juice and a very little French mustard; spread thin slices of graham bread very lightly with butter; then put a layer of the mixture; cover with another slice of buttered bread and cut into strips or squares.

RUSSIAN SANDWICHES.

Spread zephyrettes (crackers) with thin slices of cream cheese; cover with chopped olives mixed with mayonnaise. Place a zephyrette over each and press togethe

CAKES AND ICINGS.

CAKES.

Thin cakes require a hotter oven than those baked
in thick loaves. Cakes with molasses in them burn
more quickly than others. Thin cakes should bake
from fifteen to twenty minutes, thicker cakes from
thirty to forty minutes, and very thick loaves about
one hour. If only the yolks of the eggs are used the
cake is richer, if only the whites it is lighter. Have
all ingredients ready, then see that fire and oven are
right, and mix carefully. The secret of fine grained
cake is in the mixing. First always cream the butter
by beating, then add sugar slowly, creaming carefully,
then add the well beaten yolks of eggs. Sift the flour
and baking powder together three times, at least, then
add alternately in small quantities the flour and milk,
and last of all the stiffly beaten whites of eggs, work-
ing them in as lightly as possible.

ONE EGG CAKE.

Cream one half cupful of butter in a warm bowl
adding slowly one cupful of sugar, whip the yolk of
one egg and add to butter and sugar. Have ready two
cupfuls of flour into which has been sifted two teaspoonfuls of baking powder; put flour and baking
powder through sifter three times. Add flour and

one cupful of milk slowly and alternately to butter
mixture, adding last of all the whites of egg beaten
stiff and one teaspoonful of flavoring. Bake in loaf in
moderate oven for thirty minutes.

ORANGE CAKE.

Cream one third cupful of butter with one and one
half cupfuls of sugar; add the well beaten yolks of
three eggs and one teaspoonful of flavoring, beat well;
add alternately, in small quantities, two heaping cupfuls of flour, into which two rounded teaspoonfuls of
baking powder has been sifted, and one cupful of
milk; last of all add the whites of the three eggs,
beaten to a stiff froth, folding them into the dough
lightly. Bake in shallow pans for about twenty minutes, or until cake shrinks from the pan. Put together
with orange icing.

IDA'S CAKE.

Beat the whites of four eggs very stiff and set in
refrigerator to chill; cream the yolks; add one cupful
of sugar and a teaspoonful of lemon extract; sift flour
until very light, and sprinkle in one cupful slowly,
stirring lightly; then fold in the whites of the eggs as
delicately as possible. Bake in moderate oven.

ANGEL FOOD.

Sift one cupful of flour and one half teaspoonful of
cream of tartar together, sifting at least six times;
add one cupful of sugar, sift again; beat the whites
of seven eggs stiff; chill; then whip in the flour and

sugar; flavor with one teaspoonful of vanilla extract. Bake in moderate oven.

WATER SPONGE CAKE.

Beat the yolk of one egg, add one half cupful of sugar and beat again, add one half teaspoonful of lemon juice and three tablespoonfuls of cold water, then two thirds of a cupful of flour into which one half even teaspoonful of baking powder has been sifted, and lastly the whites of the egg beaten stiff. Bake in shallow pan or in small tins.

TEA CAKES.

Tea cakes that are much esteemed in southern households are made from the yolks of six eggs, half a pound of butter, one pound of sugar, one pound of flour and one teaspoonful of baking powder mixed with the flour. They should be rolled thin and baked in a quick oven. Frost with a thin icing or sprinkle while hot with granulated sugar.

POOR MAN'S CAKE.

Take three good-sized apples, pare, chop them fine, put them into a saucepan with two cupfuls of mo-lasses, and boil until the apples are soft—say for three minutes—remove, and add one cupful of sugar, one egg, and one half teaspoonful of ginger, cinnamon allspice, clove and nutmeg, one cupful of strong coffee in which one and one half teaspoonfuls of soda are dissolved; two and one half cupfuls of flour.

This cake will keep all winter. These proportions make three large cakes.

COFFEE CAKE..

One cupful of brown sugar, one cupful of molasses, one half a cupful of butter, one beaten egg, one half a cupful of strong coffee, one tablespoonful of ground cinnamon, one teaspoonful of ground cloves, four cupfuls of seeded raisins, one cupful of thinly sliced citron, four cupfuls of flour into which has been sifted one teaspoonful of soda. Bake in moderate oven.

CREAM CAKE.

Dissolve one half teaspoonful of soda and mix with one scant cupful of sour cream, beat one egg and stir in, add a scant cupful of sugar and one and one half cupfuls of flour. This can be baked as a loaf, or in gem pans, or used for layer cake.

FRIED CAKES.

Two cupfuls of sugar, four eggs, one cupful of sour cream, and one cupful of buttermilk, one teaspoonful of soda, nutmeg to taste, flour enough to make a soft dough; roll until one half inch thick, cut in rounds, cutting out small ring in center; fry in hot cocoanut butter. The fat should be deep enough to float the cakes and hot enough to cook quickly; when nicely browned, drain, then powder with confectioner's sugar.

SUGAR COOKIES.

Mix one half cupful of creamed butter with one cupful of sugar, beat to a smooth cream. Whip one egg light and add to sugar and butter; add one teaspoonful of flavoring and one fourth cupful of milk with flour enough to make sufficiently stiff to roll thin, having previously sifted through the flour one half teaspoonful of baking powder. Roll a little at a time, cut out and bake about ten minutes in hot oven.

JUMBLES.

Two eggs, six tablespoonfuls of butter, six tablespoonfuls of sugar, one teaspoonful of lemon extract, a pinch of soda sifted in flour enough to make a dough stiff enough to roll. Roll very thin, cut and bake in quick oven.

GINGER SNAPS.

To one cupful of molasses add one half a cupful of water, in which has been dissolved one teaspoonful of soda; one cupful of sugar, one teaspoonful of ginger, one teaspoonful of cinnamon, one cupful of butter with flour enough to roll. Cut and bake in quick oven.

SOFT GINGERBREAD.

Dissolve one teaspoonful of soda in four tablespoonfuls of hot water, mix with three fourths of a cupful of molasses; add four tablespoonfuls of melted butter and one and three fourths cupfuls of flour with ginger enough to flavor; bake in gem tins.

MACAROONS.

One pound of sweet almonds blanched and beaten to a paste; mix with them one and a quarter pounds of powdered sugar, the grated rind of two lemons and the whites of six eggs. Drop on buttered paper and bake a light brown in a moderate oven.

LADY FINGERS, NO. 1.

Beat two eggs until light; add one teacupful of sugar, a little salt, and flavoring to taste. Use one tea-cupful of flour sifted with one teaspoonful of baking powder, making the dough of a consistency that can be rolled. Cut into strips the size of the finger and bake.

LADY FINGERS, No. 2.

One half pint whites of eggs, beaten very stiff; add gradually one half pound sugar, beating well all the time, add the yolks of the eggs and mix together light-ly; then stir in very lightly one half pound of flour. Transfer the mixture into fingers on sheets of paper. Dust with powdered sugar, and put on pans and bake in hot oven. Watch them very carefully, as it only takes a few minutes to bake them. When cold they may be removed from the paper by placing them on the table face down, and washing the bottom of the paper with a wet sponge. Now turn back to their proper position and they can be easily removed. Join them in pairs and keep them covered until used.

ÉCLAIRS.

Put into an enameled saucepan one quarter pound of butter, one quarter pint of water, and a few drops of lemon juice; bring all to a boil; while boiling mix in smoothly one quarter pound of flour, draw back the

saucepan from the fire and add to the mixture three
well beaten eggs. Bake on greased tins in hot oven
about twenty minutes. When done make a slit in
side of each and quickly fill with either thick custard,
or stiff whipped cream that has been sweetened and
flavored; then as quickly as possible pour some chocolate frosting over the top. Serve when cold.

CREAM PUFFS.

Boil with a large cupful of hot water half a teacupful of butter, stirring in one teacupful of flour during
the boiling; set aside to cool and when cold stir in four
eggs, one at a time without beating; drop on tins
quickly and bake in a fairly hot oven. When baked
fill in with a cream made by beating together three
tablespoonfuls of flour, one egg, and half a teacupful
or more of sugar, according to taste; stirred into half
a pint of milk while boiling, and flavored to liking.

FRUIT JUMBLES.

Beat to a cream one cupful of butter; add gradually
one and one half cupfuls of sugar, the yolks of three
eggs beaten, one teaspoonful of ground cinnamon, one
half teaspoonful of ground cloves, one half a nutmeg,
grated, the juice and rind of one lemon, three tablespoonfuls of sour milk, in which has been mixed three
fourths teaspoonful of soda; one cupful of seeded and
chopped raisins, the beaten whites of three eggs, and
about three and one half cupfuls of flour; either roll
and cut out, or drop by the spoonful on a buttered
sheet.

CHOCOLATE STRIPS..

Cream three tablespoonfuls of butter, add gradually one cupful of sugar, add three tablespoonfuls of melted chocolate, one teaspoonful of vanilla and one cupful of flour, beat thoroughly, spread very thin on well buttered pans, bake in a quick oven, brush with the white of egg as soon as you take from the oven, cut into strips one inch wide while hot.

MISS FARMER'S SPONGE CAKE.

Beat the yolks of four eggs until thick, add gradually one cupful of sugar, and beat for two minutes; add three tablespoonfuls of cold water, mix and sift thoroughly one and one half tablespoonfuls of corn starch, one scant cupful of flour, one level teaspoonful of baking powder, one fourth teaspoonful of salt; add to the first mixture the whites of four eggs beaten stiff, and one teaspoonful extract of lemon. Bake in a buttered angel cake pan for forty-five minutes, or in a shallow cake-pan for thirty-five minutes in a moderate oven.

VELVET CAKE.

Cream one half cupful of butter, add gradually one and one half cupfuls of sugar, add three egg yolks well beaten and one half cupful of cold water, mix and sift thoroughly one and one half cupfuls of flour, one half cupful of corn starch, two level teaspoonfuls of baking powder; add with the beaten whites of four eggs; cover with opera caramel frosting.

ICINGS.

SOFT FROSTING.

Boil one cupful of sugar and one third cupful of water until it will string, pour slowly on the beaten white of one egg, beating constantly until cool; flavor to taste.

CREAM ICING.

Two tablespoonfuls of cream and one half teaspoonful of flavoring, add sufficient confectioners' sugar to make stiff enough to spread. Any kind of fruit juice may be used instead of cream. Orange is very nice.

ORANGE ICING.

Yolk of one egg, grated rind and juice of one orange; confectioners' sugar to make thick enough to spread.

OPERA CARAMEL FROSTING.

Cook one and one half cupfuls of brown sugar, three fourths cupful of thin cream and one half tablespoonful of butter until a ball is formed, when the mixture is tried in cold water. Beat until ready to spread.

DESSERTS.

PASTRY.

Sift one cupful of flour and one saltspoonful of baking powder together. Rub in two tablespoonfuls of shortening, mix quite stiff with ice water, using about one fourth cupful. Turn out on a floured board, pat, and roll till one fourth inch thick, then distribute one teaspoonful of butter over the surface. Sprinkle with flour and fold over and over, roll out again into a long strip, then roll like a jelly roll, and cut from end as needed, and roll out from end. The secret of good pastry is to thoroughly chill material.

For all fruit and custard pies brush bottom crust with white of egg before putting in filling. The crust will then remain dry and delicate.

A RICH PUFF PASTE.

One quart of flour and one pound of butter; sift the flour and work in the yolk of an egg well beaten; mix with ice water and roll out to the thickness of an inch or less. After the butter has been worked in cold water to extract the salt, place it on one half of the dough, folding the other half over it, set away for fifteen minutes in an ice chest, or other equally cold place, and then roll out into a long strip, which fold into three parts by turning over each end and rolling each fold; repeat this operation six or seven times. The colder the dough can be kept while being worked in this way, the better will be the results.

MINCE PIES.

To one cupful of water add one cupful of molasses, one cupful of sugar, one beaten egg, one cupful of vinegar, two and one half Boston crackers, rolled fine, one cupful of stoned raisins, butter the size of an egg, one quarter of a teaspoonful of cloves; two thirds of a teaspoonful of cinnamon; two thirds of a teaspoonful of allspice.

This will make three pies. The pies should bake slowly, taking about three quarters of an hour. A grating of nutmeg should be added to each pie before putting on upper crust. The egg, cracker, and slow baking thickens this apperently thin mixture.

FRUIT PIE.

Carefully wash two thirds of a cupful of dried currants, add equal quantity of seeded raisins; with one cupful of sugar and one cupful of water; place in saucepan and boil gently for one half hour; remove from the fire and add two tablespoonfuls of vinegar, with cinnamon, cloves, allspice, and nutmeg to taste; two chopped apples, one tablespoonful of rolled crackers, half a cupful of chopped, sweet pickled peaches, or any preserved or spiced fruit; bake with two crusts. This will make two pies.

CREAM PIE

Make a boiled custard, with one pint of milk, yolks of two eggs well beaten, and three tablespoonfuls of sugar, place in double boiler and thicken with one tablespoonful of flour that has been blended with melted butter, add one half teaspoonful of vanilla, let cook until flour is thoroughly done (if too thick a little more milk can be added). Have ready a baked pastry, fill with the mixture; then whip the whites of the two eggs to a very stiff froth and add one half cupful sugar and a few drops of flavoring, spread over the pie; set in oven just long enough to set the frosting and touch it with delicate brown. Serve cold. A chocolate pie can be made after the same method by omitting the yolks of the eggs and beating into hot milk one-fourth cake of chocolate.

CUSTARD PIE.

Beat three eggs until light, add three tablespoonfuls of sugar and beat again. Then grate sufficient nutmeg to flavor, and add three cupfuls of scalded milk. Bake slowly in single crust; as soon as the custard puffs and a knife blade can be dipped in and comes out clean, it is done.

LEMON PIE.

Beat the yolks of three eggs until thick, add one cupful of sugar and the grated yellow rind of one large lemon (be very careful not to grate any of the white of the lemon skin or it will make pie bitter), also the juice; beat until thick and light colored, then add one tablespoonful of corn starch, dissolved in a little water. Pour into a pie shell and bake slowly until it puffs. Beat the whites of the eggs until light, then gradually add three tablespoonfuls of sugar and beat until stiff. When the pie is slightly cooled, cover with this frosting, return to oven, and let it get a very delicate brown. Serve cold.

SQUASH PIE.

To one and one half cupfuls of prepared squash, add one cupful of scalded milk, one half cupful of sugar, one saltspoonful of cinnamon, a dash of nutmeg and cloves, and one egg well beaten, pour in egged crust, and bake thirty minutes, or until it puffs up all over. Sweet potato may be used in place of squash. To prepare squash or sweet potato, steam and mash.

RIPE CURRANT PIE.

To one cupful of the fruit, washed and removed from stems, add one cupful of sugar; one cupful of cream, and one tablespoonful of flour; bake with only an under crust.

NEUFCHATEL CHEESE PIE.

One Neufchatel cheese, one teacupful of sugar, grate the rind of one lemon and use with it one half of the juice, half a teacupful each of rolled cracker crumbs, and currants, four eggs, one tablespoonful melted butter, half a teacupful of cream, or rich milk,

half a nutmeg grated and one saltspoonful of salt.
Crumble the cheese and cracker crumbs well together,
beat the eggs with the sugar and add to cracker mixture, following with the butter and cream. If the
cream is very rich the butter may be omitted. Lastly,
add lemon, nutmeg and currants. The currants
should previously be washed, dried and dusted with
flour. Mix all well together and put into well buttered patty-pans that have been lined with puff-paste.
Bake fifteen or twenty minutes in a quick oven. They
will puff up, but must not be permitted to get too
brown.

PINE-APPLE TART.

Line a pie plate with pastry, and fill with mixture
made of one ounce of butter, and one half cupful of
sugar beaten to a cream; the well beaten yolks of five
eggs, a grated pineapple, one teacupful of cream and
add last of all the whites of the eggs beaten stiff and
folded in lightly, with a little more sugar.

ALMOND PEACH PIE.

Line a pie dish with puff or good plain paste; lay
halves of canned peaches, with the stone side up all
over the bottom of the crust; fill the cavity where the
pit was with a spoonful of chopped almonds; sprinkle
with sugar and pour over a very little of the peach
juice; cover with a crust, and bake till a nice brown;
serve with, or without cream;

PUDDINGS.

IRISH MOSS JELLY.

Pick over and wash carefully one half cupful of Irish Moss. Put it into one pint of boiling water, add the thin yellow rind cut from one lemon, and one cupful of sugar; simmer until the moss is dissolved, add the juice of lemon and a grating of nutmeg, and strain into a cold, wet, mould. Set away to harden; serve plain, or with cream. Orange may be used in place of lemon, though a dessert spoonful of lemon juice used with the orange improves the flavor. This Irish Moss may be substituted in place of gelatine in all delicate puddings calling for that animal product; it is to be had at any druggist's.

SAGO MILK.

Soak a cupful of sago in a quart of cold milk; put in a double boiler with one cupful of sugar; cook until the sago is dissolved; pour it into a dish, and stir in ten drops of the essence of lemon or vanilla. Serve it hot or cold.

SAGO JELLY.

Soak a cupful of sago in a quart of cold water over night; boil in double boiler for an hour; then uncover it for the water to boil away. Add two cupfuls of sugar and the strained juice of a lemon; pour it into a dish in which it may be served. Serve it cold, with smooth fresh cream, sweetened and flavored.

ORANGE FOAM (FOR TWELVE PERSONS).

To the juice of twelve oranges (the small, tart ones are best) add the juice of one lemon, the grated yellow rind of two oranges, and three cupfuls of sugar. Whip till very light the yolks of twelve eggs; then whip in the prepared juice. Whip the whites of eggs as stiff as possible (keep them well chilled while whipping) and beat in lightly, yet thoroughly, the prepared mixture. Serve in punch glasses with lady fingers. Place half of a lady finger in bottom of each glass. The amount of sugar used may vary according to the flavor of the oranges. If the foam is not stiff, then add more whites of eggs. It is difficult to give exact quantities because the flavor and juiciness of the fruit varies so. This should be prepared just before serving.

NEAPOLITAN PUDDING.

Dissolve a cupful of currant jelly in a cupful of hot water; thicken with dissolved corn starch (be careful not to use too much corn starch, only just enough to make it stiff when chilled). Have ready a chilled mold, pour in the mixture as soon as the starch is thoroughly cooked, and the white of one egg, whipped till very stiff, is added to the mixture. Then make an equal quantity of strong sweet lemonade, bringing this to a scald, thicken the same way, adding egg in same manner; pour this as second layer in mold. Then take two cupfuls of milk, bring to a scald, sweeten, and thicken as before, then add the yolks of two eggs, well beaten, whipping in one half teaspoonful of vanilla flavoring.

add to previous layers in mould (the layers can be placed in order to suit fancy), set away to chill thoroughly, and serve with whipped or plain cream. Other fruit flavors can be used in same way—pineapple or apricot syrups are very nice.

FRUIT MANGE.

To one pint of boiling water, add the juice of two nice, though any sauce may be used—brought to a scald, add one tablespoonful dissolved corn starch with sugar to taste; let boil until starch is well cooked, remove from stove and add the whites of two eggs, beaten stiff; pour into wet mould, and chill. Serve with cream and sugar.

LEMON SNOW.

To one pint of boiling water, add the juice of two lemons, and two tablespoonfuls of corn starch, well mixed with one and one fourth cupfuls of sugar; strain, and cook until thick. When partly cooled, beat vigorously with a wire egg beater or spoon, add the whites of three eggs, beaten to a stiff froth, whip in thoroughly, and pour into a chilled, wet mould; when firm and cold, turn out and serve with cold boiled custard and jelly, or cream and sugar.

ORANGE SOUFFLÉ.

Make a boiled custard with the yolks of five eggs, a quart of milk, and sugar to taste. When cool pour it over four sliced oranges, from which all seeds and tough fibre have been removed, and to which has been added one cupful of sugar, and grated rind of one orange. Place this in baking dish, cover with a meringue made of the whites of four eggs; then place the dish in a shallow pan of cold water and put in oven until the meringue is a golden brown. Serve cold.

ORANGE CUSTARDS.

Beat the yolks of six eggs with one and one half cupfuls granulated sugar till light; add to this two cupfuls of orange juice, the juice of one lemon, and the grated peel of one orange; fill in small cupfuls and place in steamer, when solid set away to chill; serve on boiled rice, over which pour a pint of rich cream, sweetened and flavored with a little grated peel of orange.

CHESTNUT CREAM.

Roast the chestnuts, then grate to powdered flakes, heaping lightly in middle of pudding dish, surround with apricot jam, and serve with whipped cream.

PEACH CAKE.

Have sponge or plain cake baked in two layers; cut or slice canned peaches; cover a layer of the cake with the cut peaches; put on another layer of cake and more peaches and turn over all well sweetened and flavored whipped cream.

STEAMED CABINET PUDDING.

Use one tablespoonful of butter to grease a three pint pudding mould. Take one cupful of fruit; raisins, candied cherries, or preserved fruits, as you prefer;

sprinkle one half the fruit in the buttered mould, then break in stale cake or bread crumbs, mixing with it the rest of the fruit, filling the mould lightly. Then whip up three eggs, add to them three tablespoonfuls of sugar and three cupfuls of milk, pour over the cake and fruit mixture. Let stand one hour, then steam for one and one fourth hours. Serve hot with creamy sauce.

COLD CABINET PUDDING.

Make a custard of one pint hot milk, yolks of three eggs, three tablespoonfuls of sugar; thicken with corn starch. Flavor with teaspoonful of vanilla. Decorate a mould with candied fruit; cover fruit with custard; cool, add a layer of lady fingers or stale cake, then a layer of fruit and more custard, and chill; continue until the mould is full. Serve with whipped cream and candied cherries.

PRUNE WHIP.

Wash thoroughly one half pound of prunes and soak three hours in enough water to cover; cook in same water until the consistency of marmalade. Rub through a sieve, sweeten. Whip the whites of four eggs, and add the prunes (which should be thoroughly chilled); beat until well mixed; pile lightly on a but tered platter, and bake until a delicate brown. Serve with whipped cream or soft custard.

WASHINGTON PIE, CHOCOLATE FILLING.

Make a plain cup cake, and bake in two layers. For the filling, beat the yolks of two eggs till light.

and add one half cupful of sugar; stir this into one half cupful of milk; melt two ounces of chocolate and stir into the milk; put on stove, and cook till it thickens; beat till cool, flavor with vanilla and spread on the cake between layers and sprinkle confectioners' sugar on top. Plain Washington pie has simply a dressing of whipped cream, sweetened, and flavored with vanilla, between the layers.

STRAWBERRY CREAM CAKE.

Make cake the same as for any good layer cake. For the filling take one cupful of thick sweet cream, whip until stiff, add four tablespoonfuls of fine grained granulated sugar and one pint of strawberries, crushed slightly, and sweetened. When cake is perfectly cold spread between layers. This should not stand long before serving.

CHARLOTTE RUSSE PIE.

Three eggs, one and one half cupfuls of sugar, two cupfuls of flour, one teaspoonful of pure cream of tartar, one half cupful of cold water, one half teaspoonful of soda. Beat the eggs thoroughly with the sugar, add one cupful of flour with even teaspoonful of pure cream of tartar, then water, and another cupful of flour. Enough for two pies.

Filling—Pure, sweet cream, beaten until stiff; sweetened to taste; flavored with vanilla. Cut open pie, fill, and pile some cream on top. Two cupfuls of cream will fill two pies.

STEAMED FRUIT PUDDING.

Make a dough of six heaping tablespoonfuls of flour; pinch of salt, one heaping teaspoonful of baking powder, two tablespoonfuls of cream, and water enough to make a soft dough; mix as lightly as possible. Then add one pint of any preserved or stewed fruit that is desired, the fruit should be well sweetened; steam for forty minutes. Be particular to keep the steam at regular heat, not letting it die down. Serve with syrup, made of the fruit juice, or hard sauce.

CHARLOTTE RUSSE.

One quart of rich, sweet, cream; whipped to a stiff foam; sweeten, after whipping, with two tablespoonfuls of sugar, and flavor with scant teaspoonful of vanilla extract. Line a glass bowl with separated lady fingers, and heap the whipped cream lightly in the bowl. Chill, and serve within an hour.

CONNECTICUT INDIAN PUDDING.

Add to three tablespoonfuls of cornmeal, three fourths of a cupful of molasses and a little salt; mix well; put one generous quart of milk in double boiler; when scalding hot add the meal and molasses; stir till free from lumps; let cook for five minutes; then butter well a baking dish, grate the rind of two or three oranges; put a layer on the bottom of the dish; pour in the liquid and put the rest of the grated peel on top; add one tablespoonful of butter to one fourth cupful hot milk; pour over pudding; bake three hours in a moderate oven; eat with rich cream, or hard sauce.

CHINESE PUDDING.

Whip one pint of cream and set it in a pan of cracked ice; add one half cupful of chopped preserved ginger, one half cupful powdered sugar; one half cupful of cold boiled rice.

Dissolve one half cupful of Irish moss in boiling water, using as little water as possible; strain, and stir into the cream mixture; stir until it thickens. Set away to harden, and serve with ginger sauce

BANANA PUDDING.

Make one quart of strong sweet lemonade, bring to a scalding point, add juice of one orange. Thicken with dissolved cornstarch, the same as any cornstarch pudding; being careful not to make too stiff. Have ready the whites of two eggs, beaten very stiff. When the corn starch is thoroughly cooked, set the dish off the stove and whip in the eggs. Then slice in two bananas, pour in moulds, set away to chill thoroughly, serve with cream and sugar. This is quite as delicious as any gelatine pudding.

CREAM RICE PUDDING.

Two cupfuls of milk, two tablespoonfuls of rice, two tablespoonfuls of sugar, one half saltspoonful grated nutmeg, one half cupful stoned raisins. Stir frequently. When it begins to thicken add more milk,

sweetened and spiced; when rice is tender add one
half cupful cream and remove from oven. Serve cold.

SWEET POTATO PUDDING.

Peel and grate the potatoes. To one quart of them
add two eggs, two tablespoonfuls of butter, three
fourths of a cupful of sugar and one cupful of sweet
milk. Cream the butter and sugar, add the eggs, stir
well, then add the other ingredients, stirring briskly.
Bake one hour. Serve hot without sauce.

OAT MEAL PUDDING.

To one cupful of cold boiled oatmeal, add one cupful of sugar, three cupfuls of milk, two well beaten
eggs, one tablespoonful of vanilla and one half cupful
of seeded raisins; bake in moderate oven about three
quarters of an hour.

SNOW BALLS.

Cook one cupful of rice until tender. Wring small
pudding cloths (one third yard square) out of hot
water and lay over a small bowl. Spread rice one
third of an inch thick over cloth. Put an apricot in
the center, filling in each half of apricot with rice.
Tie tightly and steam ten minutes. Remove the cloth
carefully and turn the balls out on a platter, and serve
with apricot sauce. Canned apricots may be used.
If fresh fruit is preferred steam the apricots tender
before removing stones.

CREAM PUDDING.

Stir together one pint of cream, three ounces of sugar, the well beaten yolks of three eggs, with scant teaspoonful of vanilla flavoring. Whip the whites of the eggs very light and add last, stirring lightly. Pour into baking dish that has been well buttered and upon which has been sprinkled bread crumbs to the thickness of ordinary pie crust. Sprinkle bread crumbs over the top of pudding, set dish in shallow pan half filled with water, and bake the same as any custard.

FRENCH BREAD PUDDING.

Butter small thin squares of bread and spread with jam, or tart jelly; place them in a buttered pudding dish; have the dish about one half full; pour over a boiled custard (using the yolks only for the custard); beat the whites of two eggs, adding gradually two tablespoonfuls of powdered sugar; beat one large tablespoonful of the jam or jelly used; heap on top of the custard and brown slightly in the oven.

SAUCES FOR PUDDINGS.

APRICOT SAUCE.

Take one cupful of apricot juice, thicken with one teaspoonful of corn starch and sweeten with one half cupful of sugar; let boil until clear.

HARD SAUCE.

Beat together one half cupful of butter and one cupful of sugar until it is creamy and white; flavor with one teaspoonful of vanilla extract.

CREAMY SAUCE.

Cream one half cupful of butter, then stir in one cupful of powdered sugar, a little at a time, and beat until very light. Then add one fourth cupful of cream or milk and one scant teaspoonful of vanilla flavoring. Just before serving set the bowl in a pan of hot water, and as soon as the sauce is smooth and creamy remove from fire. It should not be heated enough to melt the sugar.

GINGER SAUCE.

Chop finely one fourth cupful of preserved ginger; add one cupful of water and a quarter cupful of sugar, and boil for five minutes. Pour it over the well beaten whites of two eggs, add two tablespoonfuls of lemon juice, and chill.

CURRENT JELLY SAUCE.

Put four tablespoonfuls currant jelly in a saucepan with one teaspoonful of butter; let it heat and melt slowly; pour over one half cupful of boiling water, moisten one teaspoonful of cornstarch with a little cold water; add to the other ingredients and cook five minutes; add the juice of one orange, grated peel of one half orange and one and one half tablespoonfuls blanched almonds finely chopped.

EGG SAUCE.

One cupful of sugar, a tablespoonful of butter, two eggs, a little salt, and a teaspoonful of vanilla, or any flavoring preferred. Mix the butter and sugar to a cream, add the yolks of the eggs, and beat until very light. Beat the whites to a stiff froth and stir in, add flavoring and beat well together. This is especially good for apple or berry dumplings. Lemon is nice to flavor it when used for apple puddings, but should not be used for other fruits. When a plainer sauce is desired, leave out the butter.

APPLE DESSERTS.

STEAMED APPLES.

Wash, pare, and remove cores of six tart apples; place in earthen dish and put in steamer, over boiling water. Steam until soft. Serve with steamed oatmeal or boiled rice, and cream and sugar.

BAKED APPLES.

Wash, and core sour apples. Place them in earthen or granite dish and fill the center of each apple with sugar. Measure one tablespoonful of water for each apple and pour around the apples (not over, as you should not disturb the sugar in apple centers). Bake until tender, remove apples to the dish in which they will be served at table. Strain the juice, add one third cupful of sugar. Cook five minutes, and pour it over the apples, let cool, and serve with cream.

APPLE FRITTERS.

Core, pare, and cut apple into slices one fourth inch thick, sprinkle with sugar and cinnamon or nutmeg, and set them aside while making batter.

Beat the yolks of two eggs, add one tablespoonful sugar, one half cupful of sweet milk, and enough flour to make it almost a drop batter. Melt one tablespoonful of butter and add to mixture. Beat in the well whipped whites of two eggs. Dip each slice of apple into the batter, see that it is well covered and quickly drop into a kettle in which is sufficient hot cocoa butter or vegetable oil to float it; fry until the apple is soft, and the fritter a light brown on both sides. Drain, trim, and sprinkle with pulverized sugar. Serve hot.

APPLE DUMPLINGS BAKED.

Select moderate sized, tart apples; pare, core, and steam until tender, not soft; have ready a plain pie crust rolled thin in pieces size of small pie plate. Place one apple on each piece of crust, fill the core with sugar, spice to taste and add teaspoonful of hot water to sugar. Wrap crust about the apple pinching it together, place in hot oven and bake until crust is well cooked; serve hot with hard sauce.

APPLE SLUMP.

Cut apples as for pies and fill a rich undercrust of a good thickness; cover with a thick topcrust and bake in a slow oven for about an hour; when baked remove the top crust, add sugar and spice, and butter half the size of an egg, mix with the apple; then remove part of the apple. Place the top crust in an inverted way upon what remains, and the apple that has been taken out on top of that. Should be eaten hot.

APPLE RICE.

Fill a pudding dish half full with tart apples, pared, quartered, and sprinkled thickly with sugar, and a grating of nutmeg. Wash thoroughly half a cupful of rice and sprinkle over apples in pudding dish. Steam until rice is tender. Serve with cream and sugar.

APPLE CREAM.

Place in an enamelled pan with a wineglassful of water, one pound and a half of minced apple, half a pound of pulverized sugar, the finely minced rind of half a lemon, and a quarter of an ounce of ginger powder; simmer gently till soft enough to pass through a sieve. When cold, beat in thoroughly one pint of cold fresh cream, or new milk which has previously been brought to a boil, and sweetened.

APPLE FLUMMERY.

To two pounds of peeled and cored apples add one pound of sugar, and the minced rind of a fresh lemon;

place in an enamelled pan, cover with water and steam till quite soft, strain and beat the fruit to a pulp. Boil in the strained liquor one ounce of Irish moss for fifteen minutes, strain the liquor again, and add the crushed fruit, simmer for three minutes, turn into a chilled and wet mould. Let stand until solid and well chilled. Serve with cream.

SHORT CAKES.

Take one quart of flour, one teaspoonful of salt, one pint of rich sour cream; dissolve one teaspoonful of soda in a little boiling water and stir into the cream; dissolve one tablespoonful of butter and add to cream; then stir in flour, roll out as you would for biscuit; bake in round pan in two layers, spreading butter between the layers; when baked, take apart and spread with any prepared fruits.

If preferred, sweet milk and baking powder may be used in place of the sour cream and soda. And the following is an excellent receipt:

RACHEL'S SHORT-CAKE.

Two cupfuls of flour, one third cupful of butter, two well rounded teaspoonfuls of baking powder, one cupful of milk, one half teaspoonful of salt. Roll in two layers one half inch thick, butter well between layers and on the top and bake.

STRAWBERRY FILLING.

Mash one quart of strawberries in an earthen dish, add sufficient sugar to make a rich sweetness, set the dish in the oven until the dish is heated through, butter each half of the short-cake, covering with the crushed fruit, and putting a liberal supply on top, sprinkle with pulverized sugar, and serve with cream.

ORANGE FILLING.

Get small, tart, juicy oranges, pare half dozen or more, carefully remove all the white, and slice; take out all the seeds and tough fibre; then crush with enough sugar to make very sweet.

Place in agate saucepan and set on back of range to get thoroughly hot; butter the short cake liberally and apply filling between layers and on top; serve with whipped cream.

CRANBERRY FILLING.

Wash the berries and pick them over carefully; cook in agate saucepan with water enough to float over a moderate fire; mash through a colander; then add sufficient sugar to make very rich and sweet; set back on range until sugar is thoroughly dissolved; butter short-cake liberally and apply filling between layers and on top.

PINE APPLE FILLING.

Get a ripe pineapple; pare and slice; then shred with a silver fork; cover thickly with sugar, and set away for three or four hours; then set on range in an agate kettle to heat thoroughly; butter short-cake liberally, and apply filling between layers and on top; serve with whipped cream. Canned pineapple may be used, though the fresh fruit is best.

BANANA FILLING.

Slice three bananas and one orange, grate the out-side rind of the orange and mix with one cupful of sugar, and juice of orange; pour on the sliced bananas. Butter the short-cake and fill with the fruit thus prepared. Serve plain, or with whipped cream.

ICES.

WATER ICES.

The simplest way of making fruit ices is much the best. Take one pint of water to one quart of fruit juice, sweetened to taste; and it should be remembered the sugar is less apparent in the frozen mixture than in the liquid. This proportion holds for all fruit ices, except the lemon. The lemon prepare as you would a rich lemonade, adding the well beaten whites of two eggs to each quart of the mixture. Be careful to freeze smoothly and the ices will be delicious. I especially recommend strawberry, pineapple, apricot, orange and lemon.

UNCOOKED CREAM.

To one quart of cream, add one teaspoonful of vanilla flavoring, and one cupful of sugar. If you have a freezer that stirs with the triple movement in freezing, it is unnecessary to whip the cream. Otherwise it should be partially whipped before being placed in freezer.

FRENCH CREAM.

Scald one pint of milk in double boiler; beat two eggs with one cupful of sugar until light; then whip in two tablespoonfuls of flour; turn into hot milk and stir until it thickens, cook fifteen minutes and set away to cool. When cold add one quart of whipped cream, and one cupful more of sugar with one tablespoonful of vanilla flavoring; freeze.

CHOCOLATE CREAM.

To make chocolate cream add to the above, when the custard is being prepared, one ounce of dissolved sweet chocolate that has been cooked to a gloss with one tablespoonful of boiling water and two tablespoonfuls of sugar. Omit the second cupful of sugar usually added with cream.

WACHTMEISTER PUDDING.

Fill a mould with alternate layers of sponge cake and jam,—strawberry or apricot, are preferable,—then saturate with rich cream flavored with vanilla and sweetened. Freeze in moulds. Custard may be used in place of cream.

FROZEN FRUITS.

To one pound of mashed fruit, add whites of three eggs, and one pint each of sugar and water. Make a syrup of the sugar and water; when cool, add the fruit and freeze.

With sweet fruits like oranges or raspberries, add juice of one lemon and one half cupful more of sugar. The fruit is very nice, without the addition of the eggs.

PINEAPPLE SHERBET.

To one quart of grated pineapple pulp, add juice of two lemons; dissolve one and one half pounds of sugar in one pint of water, and bring to a boil, skim and cool; when cold, add the fruit pulp, and the well whipped whites of two eggs; freeze soft.

STRAWBERRY SHERBET.

Crush a pound of picked strawberries in a basin and add a quart of water with a sliced lemon, let stand for three hours; put one and one quarter pounds of sugar into another basin, cover the basin with a cheese cloth and pour the berry juice through it. When the sugar is fully dissolved strain again. Freeze soft.

CONFECTIONS.

CANDY DOUGH.

To the white of one egg placed in a glass add equal quantity of cold water, or better yet, rich, sweet cream, and one teaspoonful of vanilla extract. Beat thoroughly; then stir in gradually enough confectioner's XXXX sugar to make stiff. Cover with damp napkin and use as needed for the following varieties:

CHOCOLATE CREAMS.

Mould small pieces of candy dough into the shape of thimbles, put them on a buttered pan or paraffine paper in a cool place to harden. Melt two squares of sweet chocolate in a saucer over a tea kettle. When the cream balls are sufficiently hard, dip them in the melted chocolate. Use two forks. Let the candies drain on the forks, then put them on the tins again to dry.

CREAM WALNUTS.

Break pieces of candy dough to the size of a nutmeg, roll them in the palm of the hand until smooth and round. Press halved walnut meats on each side, letting cream show between.

CREAM ALMONDS.

Mould almond nut into center of a small ball of

candy dough. Roll in granulated sugar and set away to dry.

CREAM NUT CAKE.

May be made by stirring chopped nuts into candy dough, then rolling into sheets about three fourths of an inch thick and cutting into squares.

CREAM DATES.

Wash and dry dates, remove the stones, and fill with candy dough, then roll in confectioner's sugar.

ORANGE CREAMS.

Take the white of one egg and an equal quantity of orange juice, and grated yellow rind of one orange, mix with confectioner's sugar until a stiff dough. Mould in shapely lumps and roll in granulated sugar. This also serves for orange flavored filling for chocolate drops. Any fruit juice can be used in this same way. Any flavor desired that cannot be obtained readily from fresh fruit can be had by using extract with white of egg and cream base.

CHOCOLATE ANNAS.

To three cupfuls of white sugar, add one cupful of milk and one fourth teaspoonful of cream of tartar, boil about nine minutes, or until it will form a soft ball when dropped into cold water; then add two squares of melted chocolate and one tablespoonful of butter. Cook one minute longer. Remove from fire, add one teaspoonful vanilla extract, beat vigorously for one minute, then pour into buttered pans. When cool mark in squares.

MOLASSES CANDY.

Two cupfuls of molasses, one cupful of sugar, one teaspoonful of vinegar, one tablespoonful of butter. Boil until it is brittle when tried in cold water. Pour in a buttered tin; when cool pull until white.

BROWN BETTIES.

Two cupfuls of brown sugar, half a cupful of milk, boil about four minutes, stirring constantly; when almost done stir in three quarters of a cupful of chopped walnuts or chopped blanched almonds; remove from the fire and stir till it grains, and looks sugary, then pour into a well oiled tin to the depth of half an inch; when it cools mark off in squares with a knife.

LEMON MINTS.

Sift a quantity of confectioner's sugar into a bowl and work into it lemon juice until all sugar is absorbed, then add water, a very little at a time, until a smooth, stiff paste is formed. A bit of the lemon peel may be grated into it. Roll into balls and flatten, placing them in the oven a moment to harden.

SOFT CARAMELS.

One quart of brown sugar, half a pint of milk, one third cupful of butter, and half a cake of chocolate. Boil about nine minutes, but not so long that you cannot pour them into the pan. Mark into squares.

BUTTER SCOTCH.

Two cupfuls of light brown sugar, one cupful of butter, one tablespoonful of lemon juice and one of water. Mix all together and boil twenty minutes, add one fourth teaspoonful of baking soda, drop a little in water and if it is crisp it is ready to take off. If not, cook longer; when done, pour into a flat buttered tin.

MARSHMALLOWS.

Three ounces of gum-arabic, half a pint of hot water, half a pint of powdered sugar, the white of one egg, flavoring. Dissolve the gum-arabic in the water, strain, and add the sugar. Boil ten minutes or until the syrup has the consistency of honey, stirring all the time. Add the egg, beaten stiff, and as soon as thoroughly mixed remove from the fire; add flavoring to taste, orange flower or rose is generally used. Pour the paste into a pan dusted with corn starch. The paste should be spread one inch thick. Cut into squares when cold, and roll in powdered sugar.

CHOC-O-POP.

Have ready a mixture made of one cupful of sugar, one half cupful of molasses and one cake of chocolate, cooked until it nearly crisps in cold water, keep warm. Pop corn enough to fill a three quart bowl, turn into a big pan and mix with the candy.

CRACKER-JACK.

Is made in the same way, only use one third sugar to two thirds molasses and omit the chocolate.

FROSTED FRUITS.

Carefully pick over and wash the fruit. such as cherries, plums or strawberries. Whip the whites of two or three eggs, according to quantity of fruit; dip the fruit in beaten egg, drain (keep the eggs well beaten) then dip fruit into powdered sugar. Cover a pan with a sheet of white paper, place the fruit on glass dish; dry, chill, and serve.

STUFFED DATES.

Wash and carefully dry the dates by placing them in a colander and letting stand in warm place; remove the stones and insert half a pecan, or one fourth of an English walnut; roll in confectioner's sugar.

SALTED ALMONDS.

Blanch half a pound of almonds by pouring over them one pint boiling water; let stand three minutes. Drain and cover with cold water. Remove the skins and dry the almonds on a towel. Fry in hot butter. Drain on brown paper, and sprinkle with salt.

BUTTER SCOTCH.

One cupful of sugar, one cupful of molasses, half a cupful of butter, nearly one tablespoonful of vinegar, a pinch of soda; boil until done; when cold, cut into squares and wrap in paraffine paper.

CARAMELS.

One cupful of molasses, one half cupful of milk, one cupful of sugar, one teaspoonful of flour, one table-spoonful of butter, one fourth pound of chocolate; boil until it will harden when dropped in cold water, then add a few drops of glycerine and one teaspoonful of vanilla; turn into a buttered pan, when partly cool, mark in squares.

COFFEE CREAM CARAMELS.

Melt two pounds of sugar with as little water as possible; when the sugar begins to bubble, pour in slowly one teacupful of rich cream and stir carefully; add two ounces of fresh butter and the extract from two ounces of coffee, stirring gently and continuously while adding. As soon as cooked sufficiently to be brittle when dropped in cold water, pour into buttered tin dish, and when nearly cooled, mark off with a buttered knife into squares.

CHOCOLATE CARAMELS.

Cream together one teacupful of sugar with half the quantity of butter; add one fourth of a pound of grated chocolate and one teacupful each of molasses and milk. Beat well together and boil until a portion of it dropped in ice-water sets and cracks. Pour into well buttered tin pans to the thickness of half an inch. When nearly cold mark into squares with a buttered knife.

LEMON CANDY.

Put one pound of sugar into a pan or kettle with half a pint of water and a third of a teaspoonful of cream of tartar; let it boil, and when a little of it dropped in cold water becomes brittle it is done; pour

into a shallow buttered dish. When cooled sufficiently to be handled add one third of a teaspoonful of
tartaric acid with the same quantity of extract of
lemon, and work thoroughly into the candy until the
acid has been evenly distributed. If worked too much
the transparency of the candy may be destroyed.

COCOANUT DROPS.

Grate one cocoanut and add to it one half its
weight in sugar and the white of an egg whipped to a
stiff froth. Mix all together thoroughly and drop on
buttered white paper in a pan. Bake for fifteen
minutes.

KISSES.

Beat the whites of four eggs to a stiff froth and stir
in half a pound of confectioner's sugar, flavor with one
half teaspoonful of vanilla. Whip thoroughly and
then drop in quantities about half the size of an egg
on buttered paper, well separated; lay the paper on a
half inch board and place in moderate oven. Watch
carefully and when they begin to color take them out,
remove from paper and join them in pairs by their flat
surfaces.

BEVERAGES.

TEA.

Tea should be made with the little filagree silver balls that come especially for that purpose. Fill ball with best quality Oolong, or English Breakfast, tea that you can obtain (cheap teas are injurious and tasteless). Have a pot of boiling water, fill your cup and then immerse the tea ball in cup until the strength desired is obtained. Serve with sugar and sliced lemon, after the Russian fashion; it is more wholesome than with cream.

COCOA.

Allow one teaspoonful of cocoa and sugar to one cupful of milk and water, in equal proportions. Heat the milk in double boiler. Put the water in the cocoa pot, when it boils stir in the dry cocoa, mix well. After boiling three minutes, add the hot milk. Serve when it begins to rise in the pot.

FRENCH COFFEE.

Three pints of water to one cupful of ground coffee. Put coffee in bowl; pour over it about half pint cold water and let stand for fifteen minutes; bring remaining water to a boil. Take coffee in bowl, strain through fine sieve, then take French coffee pot, put coffee grounds in strainer at top of French pot, leaving water in bowl. Then take boiling water and pour over coffee very slowly. Then set coffee-pot on stove for five minutes; do not let boil. Take off and pour in cold water from bowl that coffee was first soaked in, to settle. Serve in another pot. The French, who have the reputation of making the best coffee, use three parts Java to one part of Mocha.

AMERICAN COFFEE.

Allow one tablespoonful of ground coffee to each cupful of water used; mix coffee with half the white of one egg; add one cupful of cold water and shake well, then add as many more cupfuls of cold water as you have allowed for. Place on back of range and steep ten minutes, then bring forward. Let come to a boil. Settle with one half cupful of cold water.

CARAMEL COFFEE.

To prepare, take three and one half quarts of bran, add one and one half quarts of corn meal, one pint of molasses, one half pint of boiling water, mix well, and bake, stirring often. Make the same as "American Coffee," only let boil a little longer.

CHOCOLATE.

Melt dry, over steam, one half cake of sweet chocolate; bring to a scald one quart of rich milk, add one cupful of sugar, turn into a heated bowl, then add the melted chocolate and whip with egg beater until chocolate is thoroughly dissolved in the milk. The longer it is whipped the better it will be. Serve with whipped cream.

APRICOT WATER.

Skin twelve apricots, take out the stones, pour on one quart of boiling water; allow them to stew for one hour, then strain off the clear liquid and sweeten with three ounces of sugar.

GINGERADE.

Gingerade is made of any fruit, stewed with pulverized ginger, flavored with lemon juice, and carefully strained.

GRAPE JUICE.

Wash and remove from stems ten pounds of grapes, put over to boil with two quarts of water. Let boil until seeds and pulp separate. Strain through cheese cloth bag, let it drain slowly, do not squeeze. Put juice back in kettle, let come to a boil, and add one and one fourth pounds of sugar; boil two or three minutes. Seal boiling hot. The secret of success in bottling grape juice is to have everything boiling hot, jars, juice, rubbers, and tops. The best way is to have jars in kettle of boiling water right on the stove and tops in boiling water, likewise, and fill right from kettle of boiling juice on the stove. Then if your cans are airtight the juice will surely keep.

FRUIT JUICES.

The following rules hold good for any kind of fruit: Crush the small fruits raw, strain, add one half pound

of sugar to each quart of juice, let boil one minute, and
bottle, using same precautions as those specified in
receipt for grape juice.

PINEAPPLE FRAPPÉ.

Boil one quart of water, one pint of sugar, and one
pint of chopped pineapple for twenty minutes; add one
cupful of orange juice and one half cupful of lemon
juice.   Freeze soft.

ORANGE FRAPPÉ.

Make a syrup by boiling one quart of water and one
pint of sugar for twenty minutes; add one pint of
orange juice and the juice of two lemons; one cupful
of candied cherries should be added just before freezing.   Freeze soft.

ENGLISH MARMALADES.

RHUBARB MARMALADE.

Peel and cut into inch pieces tender young rhubarb, to every pint allow one pound of loaf sugar and three oranges. Spread the cut rhubarb on a shallow dish and cover with the sugar; leave it for twelve hours; then put it into the preserving kettle with the grated yellow rind of the oranges (be careful not to use any of the white pulp or it will make the preserve bitter), add the tender, juicy pulp of the oranges and boil slowly for about one hour, or until jam sets when tested on a cold plate.

ORANGE MARMALADE.

To every pound of sliced oranges (one half Seville and one half sweet) add three pints of cold water; let stand in a cool place for forty-eight hours; then boil all together until tender, generally about two hours; set away for twenty-four hours. Then weigh the fruit and to every pound of the boiled fruit add three fourths of a pound of sugar. Boil until it will "set" when tried on a chilled plate.

LEMON MARMALADE.

Pour a scant quart of boiling water over two pounds of sugar and let it stand until dissolved. Put in agate preserving kettle and peel some very thin, thread-like strips of the delicate yellow rind of the lemons; add to the liquid; carefully peel and remove all fibrous parts from six large lemons, collect the seeds, tying them in a thin cloth; add the pulp and the little bag of seeds to syrup, keep kettle uncovered and let preserve boil gently. When it "sets" on a chilled plate it is done. The seeds used in this way make it jell much more quickly and the marmalade is more delicate in flavor.

APRICOT MARMALADE.

Choose deep yellow apricots, not too ripe; take off the skin, take out the stones, and extract the kernel. To each twelve pounds of fruit add eight pounds of sugar, put in agate kettle, and boil until it will "set" by dropping into a chilled plate. It needs to be stirred frequently and carefully watched to prevent burning.

INVALID COOKERY.

PEA SOUP.

One pint of fresh, or one can of marrowfat peas; boil until thoroughly soft so they will mash easily; then strain through a sieve to remove skins. To pulp and liquor add one pint of cream, one teaspoonful of sugar, salt and pepper to taste, and one tablespoonful of butter. Serve with wafers. This is a very nutritious and relishable soup for a convalescent.

MILK TOAST.

Brown delicately a thin slice of stale bread, cut in strips and place in bowl; to one cupful of rich milk, brought to a scald, add a teaspoonful of butter, have ready one heaping teaspoonful of flour blended with water, strain into scalding milk and stir until it thickens, set back and let cook gently while you whip the white of one egg to a stiff froth, add a pinch of salt, then take the simmering milk from the stove and whip the beaten white of egg in quickly. Pour over toast in bowl and serve at once.

CUP CUSTARD.

Allow one egg and three fourths of a cupful of rich milk for each cup, sweeten to taste and flavor with grated nutmeg, or vanilla extract, as you prefer, pour in cups, set cup in shallow tin half filled with water, and place in oven; bake until solid, and knife blade can be drawn out clean. Cooking in the pan of water prevents custards from separating and becoming watery.

RICE FOAM.

Wash one heaping teaspoonful of rice and cook until thoroughly tender in milk; mash through a sieve; add pinch of salt; heat a half cupful of cream to a scald, and stir in the rice. Whip the white of one egg to a stiff froth, and add immediately on removing from the stove. A bit of chopped parsley may be added, if liked. Serve with wafers. This is a pleasant change from sweet gruels, and is very nutritious.

CREAMED GRUEL.

Cook one tablespoonful of rolled oats in scant pint of water; when soft strain through a sieve; add one half cupful of cream; salt to taste, and let come to a scald. Have ready the whites of two eggs beaten to a stiff froth, take gruel from the fire and whip in the eggs, sweeten to taste and flavor with a dash of nutmeg or a few drops of vanilla extract.

EGG GRUEL.

Heat a cupful of milk to 180 F., and stir into it one well beaten egg mixed with one fourth cupful of cold water. Stir constantly for a few minutes until thickened, but do not allow it to boil again. Season with salt, or if preferred, a little loaf sugar.

BARLEY GRUEL.

Wash three tablespoonfuls of pearl barley, drop it into a pint of boiling water and parboil five minutes. Pour the water off and add one quart of fresh boiling water, let it simmer gently from one to three hours, strain, season, and serve. A small piece of lemon rind added to the gruel one half hour before it is done will give an agreeable flavor. Equal quantities of barley gruel and milk make a very nourishing drink; a little lemon juice with sugar to taste is sometimes liked as the flavor for the gruel.

ARROWROOT.

Mix two tablespoonfuls of arrowroot with four tablespoonfuls of cold water; add half a pint of boiling water and boil until it thickens; sweeten to taste and add a little grated nutmeg.

GRAHAM GRUEL.

Mix one tablespoonful of graham meal in four tablespoonfuls of cold water, stir it into a pint of boiling water, cook twenty minutes, salt to taste, and boil ten minutes longer, put a gill of thin gruel into a cup with one half gill of milk or cream, and serve hot.

EGG NOGG.

Beat the yolk of a freshly laid egg with a tablespoonful of sugar until it is light and creamy, add to this one half cupful of milk (hot or cold, as you wish the drink, warm, or chilled), whip in, lightly, the white of the egg, beaten stiff, a light grating of nutmeg, and

if mixed cold, a tablespoonful of cracked ice. Serve
at once.

EGG AND LIME WATER.

To a wineglass full of lime water, add the stiffly
beaten white of one egg. Give this often, in small
quantities, to patient. It is excellent in cases of obsti-
nate vomiting and bowel trouble.

APPLE WATER.

Wash and wipe a large sour apple and, without
paring, cut it into thin slices. Put them in a bowl
with one strip of lemon peel, add one cupful of boiling
water, cover and set away to cool, strain when cold,
sweeten and serve with cracked ice. Cranberries or
rhubarb may be used in the same way.

EGG LEMONADE.

Beat the white of an egg to a stiff froth, mix with
it the juice of a small lemon and one tablespoonful of
sugar. Add one cupful of ice water and shake thoroughly.

ARROWROOT WATER.

Boil the thin rind of a fresh lemon in one quart of
water. When boiling, pour over one tablespoonful of
arrowroot previously mixed with a little cold water,
stir well, sweeten to taste, and let it boil for five minutes; squeeze in the juice of one lemon.

BARLEY WATER.

One teaspoonful of pearl barley, one half lemon,
one quart boiling water, sugar to taste. Wash the

barley in cold water, add boiling water, juice of lemon, a bit of rind, let stand, covered, and warm for three hours.

EGG TEA.

Take the white of one egg and beat it to a stiff froth, beat the yolk into it with a scant tablespoonful of sugar, then pour in slowly (beating the mixture all the time) half a cupful of hot milk; flavor with grated nutmeg or vanilla to taste.

TOAST WATER.

Brown nicely in the oven slices of bread, and pour upon them sufficient boiling water to cover. Let them steep until cold, keeping the bowl or dish containing the toast closely covered. Strain off the water and sweeten to taste. Chill by setting dish in bowl of chopped ice.

BARLEY WATER.

Put two ounces of pearl barley into half a pint of boiling water and let it simmer a few minutes. Drain off and add two quarts of boiling water with a few figs and stoned raisins cut fine. Boil slowly until reduced about one half and strain. Sweeten to taste, adding the juice of a lemon and nutmeg if desired.

BAKED MILK.

Put the milk in a jar, covering the opening with white paper, and bake in a moderate oven until thick as cream. May be taken by the most delicate stomach.

FLAXSEED LEMONADE.

Pour on four tablespoonfuls of whole flaxseed one quart of boiling water and add the juice of two lemons. Let it steep for three hours, keeping it closely covered. Strain and sweeten to taste.

IMPORTANT NOTES.

THE WAY TO TEST HOT FAT.

If a bit of dry bread will brown in one minute fat is hot enough for a raw mixture. If cooked mixtures are to be browned the fat should be hot enough to brown a piece of bread in forty seconds. This method however, is only a makeshift and is not absolutely accurate. A thermomoter should be used; 380 to 390 degrees is the right temperature for frying vegetable substances. Heat fat slowly.

CELERY FLAVORING.

Clean the green stalks and leaves of celery and dry, place in paper bags to be used for soups and savories when celery is out of season. This can be used in place of the celery seed called for in some receipts.

NUT BUTTER.

Peanuts shelled and well roasted with the skins rubbed off will, when ground, dissolve into a buttery substance which can be spread on bread and made into sandwiches. All kinds of nuts reduced to flour can be readily digested and can be placed on the table to be eaten with bread or spread on sandwiches.

BAY LEAVES.

Bay leaves contribute a most delicate and pungent flavor to soups, savories and gravies. They can be obtained at any druggist's, and five cents worth will last a long time.

SUBSTITUTES FOR INGREDIENTS IN NON-VEGETARIAN RECEIPTS.

SUET.

In place of suet use bread crumbs soaked in oil or butter.

MEATS.

Use nuts as substitute for meats. To prepare the nuts for cooking, pick from the shell carefully and chop very fine, or better yet, grind in nut mill.

GELATINE.

In place of gelatine, use Irish Moss or corn starch.

MEAT FATS.

Nut butter takes the place of meat extract and fats in gravies and sauces. Where plain butter is preferred with a savory flavoring of herbs, always brown the flour used for thickening.

PASTRY.

Cocoanut or cow's butter is the substitute for lard or cotoline in vegetarian pastry.

HERBS.

The value of herbs for savories and soups is too little understood by American cooks. Here is "Aunt Susan's" receipt for a "soup powder" that will flavor any soup, gravy, or savory dish with a fine flavor:

SOUP POWDER.

Sweet Marjoram—Powdered, two ounces.
Parsley—Powdered, two ounces.
Summer Savory—Powdered, two ounces.
Thyme—Powdered, two ounces.
Bay Leaf—Powdered, two ounces.
Lemon Peel—Powdered, one ounce.
Sweet Basil—Powdered, one ounce.
Rosemary—Powdered, one ounce.

TO PREPARE ONIONS FOR SALADS OR FILLINGS.

Peel and slice, or chop, cover the onions with boiling water, and let stand three or four minutes, drain and put in ice water, let stand ten or fifteen minutes, or, until crisp. The onions are just as crisp as before, and much more delicate.

THE WAY TO DRY CORN.

Just scald, then cut from the cob, put in a pan and set over kettle of boiling water; stir frequently, and in a couple of hours the corn will be almost dry, if the water in kettle has been constantly kept at boiling. Set in warm oven half an hour and the corn is ready to put in bags; dry and clean.

WEIGHTS AND MEASURES FOR COOKS.

1 pound of wheat flour is equal to............1 quart
1 pound and two ounces of Indian meal make..1 quart
1 pound of soft butter is equal to.............1 quart
1 pound and 2 ounces of best brown sugar make 1 quart
1 pound and 1 ounce of powdered white sugar
    make ....1 quart
1 pound of broken loaf sugar is equal to......1 quart
4 large tablespoonfuls make..................½ gill
1 common-sized tumbler holds................½ pint
1 common-sized wine glass is equal to.........½ gill
1 tea-cup holds.............................. 1 gill
1 large wine glass holds....................2 ounces
1 tablespoonful is equal to.................½ ounce

COLORING FOR SAUCES AND SOUPS.

Crush a quarter of a pound of loaf sugar to powder, put it into a sauce pan with a tablespoonful of water, and stir it unceasingly over a gentle fire until it begins to acquire a little color. Draw it back and bake it very slowly, still stirring it, until it is almost black, without being in the least burnt. It will take about half an hour. Pour a quart of water over it, let it boil for a few minutes until the sugar is quite dissolved, pour it out, and when cold, strain it into a bottle and store it for use. A tablespoonful of this browning will color half a pint of liquid.

BOILING VEGETABLES.

It is very essential for health that all the proper-ties of food should be retained in the cooking, therefore the habit of boiling the various vegetables, in an unnecessary quanity of water, and then draining this down the sink, is a means of defrauding the organism of the nourshment originally contained in the article.

Potatoes, carrots, parsnips, and other articles requiring their skins to be removed for serving or mincing, should, when possible, be steamed "in their jackets" and peeled as much as necessary afterwards.

Cauliflowers, cabbage, &c., are excellent when steamed. Green peas, beans, and such, should be put in a covered vessel, with a little butter, and, when necessary, a spoonful or two of water, and gently stewed, standing inside a saucepan of water without the water touching them; or they can be stewed in the oven in an earthenware jar, with a little butter and a spoonful or two of water. This method of cooking takes very little longer time than the ordinary boiling in water. The oven should be moderately heated.

STEWING FRUITS.

Fruits are better stewed in a double enamelled saucepan, or baked in a tightly covered earthen jar in the oven with as little water as possible.

Dried fruits, such as raisins, figs, dates, &c., should be washed and picked over carefully, then soaked for several hours in cold water till they are soft and swollen to their fullest extent, when they should be stewed in the same water.

USE OF SALT.

As little salt as is palatable should be used, and an effort made to daily lessen its use. When once the system is freed from the use of this mineral in its daily food, a small dose shows it to be an active poison. There is enough of natural salts in our vegetable foods without our making use of the mineral deposit. Knowing that many will use this book who are just turning from the meat diet, we give, as a rule, the usual quantity of salt in the receipts used in ordinary cookery. For the same reason we give the ordinary beverages in daily use, in the menus.

BEVERAGES.

Fruit juices are far more conductive to good health than tea or coffee, and we especially recommend lemon juice diluted with boiling water as a breakfast beverage, though we have not ventured to place it on the regular bill of fare. It is a most appetising morning drink, and should be taken a short time before eating.

MENUS FOR ONE WEEK.

BREAKFAST—MONDAY.

Chinese Rice with Cream.　　　　　　Fruit.
Boiled Eggs.　　　Creamed Potatoes.
Whole Wheat Muffins.　　Lemon Marmalade.
Coffee.

LUNCHEON—MONDAY.

Bean Soup with Nouilles.
Toast.　　Boiled Egg Sandwiches　　Jelly.
Gingerade.

DINNER—MONDAY.

Cream of Tomato.
Steamed Sweet Potato.　　　Celery on Toast.
Macaroni and Cheese.
Lettuce with Mayonaise.　　Whole Wheat Bread.
Fruit Pie.
Stuffed Dates.　　　　　　Grape Juice.

BREAKFAST—TUESDAY.

Fruit.

Whole Wheat with Cream.   Savory Hash.

Warmed Sweet Potatoes.

Griddle Cakes.   Syrup.

Coffee.

LUNCHEON—TUESDAY.

Cabbage Soup.

Baked Potatoes.   Fried Apples.

Corn Muffins.   Preserves.

Oolong Tea.

DINNER—TUESDAY.

Soup.

Cream of Celery.

Mashed Potatoes.   Omelet with Peas.   Wax Beans.

Tomato Aspic on Lettuce

with

Mayonaise Dressing.

Cabinet Pudding.   Coffee.

BREAKFAST—WEDNESDAY.

Breakfast Food with Cream.   Stewed Raisins.

Creamed Potatoes.   Shirred Eggs.   Toast.

Tea or Coffee.

LUNCHEON—WEDNESDAY.

Dutch Soup.

Wachtmeister Potatoes.

Hot Biscuit.   Apricot Sauce.

Tea.

DINNER—WEDNESDAY.

Soup.

Cream of Carrot.

Escaloped Tomatoes.   Rice and Cheese.   Parsnip Balls.

Potato Salad.

Apricot Tapioca.   Cake.

Coffee.

BREAKFAST—THURSDAY.

Oat Meal with Cream.

Corn Fritters.   French Fried Potatoes.

Stewed Prunes.

Whole Wheat Muffins.   Tea.

LUNCHEON—THURSDAY.

Corn on Toast.

Lyonaise Potatoes.   Cheese Puffs.

Whole Wheat Bread and Butter.

Cake.   Peaches.

Cocoa.

DINNER—THURSDAY.

Clear Soup with Nouilles.

Escaloped Potatoes.   Vegetable Cutlets.   Lima Beans.

Celery Salad.

Apple Dumplings.   Hard Sauce.

Nuts and Raisins.

French Coffee.

BREAKFAST—FRIDAY.

Fruit.

Breakfast Food with Cream.

Potato Balls.   Fried Tomatoes.

Corn Cakes with Syrup.

Caramel Coffee.

LUNCHEON—FRIDAY.

Welsh Rarebit.

Baked Potatoes.   Stewed Tomatoes.

Oat Meal Pudding.

Tea.

DINNER—FRIDAY.

Corn Chowder.

Escaloped Potatoes.   Devilled Tomatoes.

Mushroom Pie.   Cheese Relish.

Banana Short Cake.   Fruit Juice.

BREAKFAST—SATURDAY.

Fruit.

Oat Meal with Cream.

Milk Toast. Baked Potatoes.

Bread Griddle Cakes. Jam.

English Breakfast Tea.

LUNCHEON—SATURDAY.

Rice Soup.

Creamed Potatoes. Escaloped Eggs.

Honey and Waffles.

Chocolate.

DINNER—SATURDAY.

Split Pea Soup.

Lyonaise Potatoes. Nut Loaf. Wax Beans.

Salad of

Lettuce and Grape Fruit.

Apple Pie. Cheese.

Coffee.

BREAKFAST—SUNDAY.

Fresh Fruit.

Porridge with Cream.

French Fried Potatoes. Boston Baked Beans.

Brown Bread.

Coffee.

DINNER—SUNDAY.

Julienne Soup.

Welsh Rarebit.

Corn on Toast.   Baked Sweet Potatoes.

Mushroom Pie.   Nut Salad.

Orange Foam.   Lady Fingers.

Coffee.

SUNDAY NIGHT LUNCH.

Russian Sandwiches.   Celery Salad.

Cake and Fruit.

Grape Juice.

MENUS FOR PLAIN LIVING.

BREAKFASTS.

Breakfast Food.   Marmalade.

Creamed Potatoes.

Whole Wheat Griddle Cakes.   Syrup.

Coffee.

Breakfast Food with Cream.

Spanish Eggs.   Rice Fritters.

Graham Gems.   Apricot Marmalade.

Tea.

Fruit.

Graham Porridge with Cream.

Corn Muffins. Vegetable Sausages.

Lyonaise Potatoes.

Chocolate.

Grapes.

Rye Porridge with Cream.

Boiled Potatoes. Vegetable Cutlets.

Whole Wheat Muffins.

Coffee.

Apples.

Whole Wheat Porridge with Cream.

Baked Potatoes. Fried Corn Mush.

Lemon Marmalade. Pop Overs.

English Breakfast Tea.

Bananas.

Oat Meal with Cream.

Potato Pancakes. Toast. Scrambled Eggs.

English Breakfast Tea.

Oranges.

Chinese Rice.

Shirred Eggs. Creamed Potatoes.

Pop Overs.

Coffee.

Porridge with Cream.

Savory Hash.

Orange Marmalade.   Muffins.

Chocolate.

Fruit.

Oat Meal Porridge with Cream.

Rice Griddle Cakes.   Maple Syrup.

Coffee.

DINNERS.

Soup.

Cream of Asparagus.

Omelet with Peas.

Lima Beans.   Creamed Potatoes.

Pop Overs.

Rice Pudding.   Coffee.

Rice Soup.

Vegetable Hash.

Escaloped Potatoes.   Cabbage Salad.

Squash Pie with Cheese.

Coffee.

Lentil Soup.
Italian Macaroni.
Corn Fritters.   Lyonaise Potatoes.
Apple Tapioca.
Coffee.

———

Baked Beans.
Stewed Tomatoes.   Baked Sweet Potatoes.
Rolls.
Apple Dumplings.   Coffee.

———

Escaloped Eggs.
Mashed Potatoes.   Corn on Toast.
Snow Pudding.
Coffee.

———

Sweet Breads with Peas.
Mashed Potatoes.   Biscuit.
Oat Meal Pudding.
Coffee.

———

Tomatoes on Toast.
Baked Potatoes.   Macaroni and Cheese.
Orange Custard on Rice.
Coffee.

Bean Puree with Nouilles.

Creamed Vegetables.   Stewed Tomatoes.

Macaroni Pie.   Cheese Puff.

Fruit.   Coffee.

Potato Soup with Dumplings.

Cheese Custard.   Wafers.

Farina Cronstades.

Potatoes in White Sauce.   Sliced Cucumbers.

Pineapple Tart.

Coffee.

COLD SUPPERS.

Egg Sandwiches.   Celery Salad with Cheese Sticks.

Coffee Cake.   Orange Foam.

Iced Tea.

Tomato Salad.   Whole Wheat Bread.

Nut Sandwiches.

Angel Food.   Strawberries and Cream.

Lemonade.

Boston Baked Beans Cold,
Serve with cut lemons.

Whole Wheat Bread. Butter.

Olives.

Cheese. Wafers.

Sliced Peaches.

Sponge Cake. Chocolate Sandwiches.

Grape Juice.

HOT SUPPERS.

Bean Salad. Wachtmeister Potatoes.

Waffles with Syrup.

Celery. Cheese. Crackers.

Coffee.

Tomato Fritters. Baked Potatoes.

Cake. Sauce.

Chocolate.

Rice Croquettes.

Lyonaise Potatoes.

Jelly. Pop Overs.

Tea.

Savory Hash. Baked Potatoes.

Tomato Salad.

Honey. Whole Wheat Muffins.

Chocolate.

FORMAL LUNCHEONS.

Cherries.

New Potatoes.   Nut Croquettes.   Steamed Corn.

Italian Salad.   Wafers.

Macaroons.   Orange Ice.   Kisses.

Chocolate with Whipped Cream.

Tomato Bouillon.

Sweet Breads Served on Green Peas.

Wachtmeister Potatoes.   Grilled Mushrooms.

Lettuce Salad.

Wafers.   Cheese.

Lady Fingers.   Eclairs.   Chocolate Stripes.

Pine-Apple Sherbert.

Soup.

Cream of Green Peas.

Eggs and Asparagus. Farina Croustades. Potato Pears.

Salad of

Grape Fruit and Walnut.

Graham Sandwiches.   Wafers.

Chocolate Cream.

Velvet Cake.   Chocolate.

Corn Soup.

An English Monkey.   Bread.

Savory Eggs.

Boiled Potatoes.   Turnip Soufflé.

Snow Balls.

Orange Cake.   Gingerade.

Oranges.*

Welsh Rarebit.

Potato Croquettes.   Fricassed Tomatoes.   Baked Eggs.

Baked Mushrooms.

Bread.   Butter.

Nut Salad.

Wachtmeister Pudding.   Grape Juice.

Macaroni Soup.

Curried Rice.   Fried Tomatoes.   Yorkshire Pudding.

Princess Potatoes.

Olives.   Salmagundi.   Wafers.

Frozen Fruits.

Coffee.

---

* Peel and pierce with a fruit fork, leaving fork in the fruit; lay on
a bed of cracked ice in shallow dish; serve from the platter.

FORMAL DINNERS.

————

Mock Turtle Soup.

Mashed Potato.   Biscuit Patês.   Lima Beans.

Cabbage Salad.

Bread.   Butter.

Olives.

Pine-apple Short Cake.

Celery.   Cheese.   Crackers.

Coffee.

————

Julienne Soup.

Vegetable Omelet.

Escaloped Potatoes.   Stuffed Tomatoes.

Italian Salad.   Wafers.

Ripe Current Pie.

Coffee.

————

Soup.

Cream of Asparagus.

Mashed Potatoes.   Nut Croquettes.   Peas.

Baked Mushrooms.

Cheese Wafers.   Tomato Salad.

Orange Short Cake.

Coffee.

Soup.
Cream of Potato.
Baked Egg Plant.   Eggs with Mushrooms.
Pastry with Peas.
Lettuce Salad.   Cheese Wafers.
Charlotte Russe.
Coffee.

———

Tomato Bouillon.
Welsh Rarebit.
New Potatoes.   Asparagus Pie.   Peas.
Tomato Salad.
Bread.   Butter.
Frozen Sherbet.
Macaroons.   Stuffed Dates.   Lady Fingers.
Coffee.

———

Soup.
Cream of Celery.
Potato Pates.   Mushroom Pie.   French Peas.
Stuffed Tomato Salad with Mayonaise.
Bread.   Butter.   Olives.
Banana Pudding.   Cakes.
Nuts.   Raisins.
Coffee.

MERCURY,

◎ ◎ ◎ ◎

A Theosophical Monthly, devoted to the study of Oriental Philosophy, the Occult Sciences and the Brotherhood of Man.   John Walters, Managing Editor.

ADDRESS

MERCURY PUBLISHING OFFICE,

414 MASON ST.,

SAN FRANCISCO,   CALIFORNIA.

Price, $1.00 a Year; 10 Cents Single Copy.

Contains 32 pages; has a special Forum department, to which readers are invited to send questions; Theosophical news; Book Reviews and a "Children's Corner." It is the official organ of the American Section of the Theosophical Society.

Volume III

~~~~OF THE~~~~

SECRET DOCTRINE.

The most wonderful esoteric work of the Twentieth Century written by

Madame H. P. Blavatsky,

founder of the Theosophical Society.

Published by

THE THEOSOPHICAL BOOK CONCERN,

Room 426 Athenaeum Building, Chicago,

AND BY THE

Theosophical Publishing Society,

LONDON, ENGLAND.

WRITE FOR INFORMATION.

Food, Home and Garden,

A Monthly Magazine edited by Rev. Henry S. Clubb.

One Subscription 50c.   Four Subscriptions $1 per year:

TO THE PUBLIC.

This publication is intended to afford information as to the best food to promote the physical, moral and spiritual welfare without destroying the lives of other sensitive creatures.

FOOD.

Its chief contention is that the fruits, nuts and grains, with a fair proportion of fresh and preserved vegetable productions (with or without the products of animals), are wholesome and pure. That flesh meat contains the germs of diseases to which animals are subject and contain the thick, venous blood, a substance so poisonous that it will cause blood poisoning whenever it comes in contact with the arterial blood of the body. That by avoiding the butcher's meat and living on the pure foods provided so abundantly in the Vegetable kingdom a higher degree of health and strength can be obtained: a longer life and greater freedom from irritation and nervous exhaustion, under pressure of business or professional labor.

The principles of humanity towards animals and the effects of pure food in promoting man's ethical and spiritual progress are also discussed in this magazine.

Philadelphia: The Vegetarian Society of America,

310 CHESTNUT STREET.

THEOSOPHICAL MANUALS.

No. 1.
THE SEVEN PRINCIPLES OF MAN.

By ANNIE BESANT.   Cloth, 35 cents.

No. 2.
RE-INCARNATION.

By ANNIE BESANT.   Cloth, 35 cents.

No. 3.
DEATH—AND AFTER?

By ANNIE BESANT.   Cloth, 35 cents.

No. 4.
KARMA.

By ANNIE BESANT.   Cloth, 35 cents.

No. 5.
THE ASTRAL PLANE.

By C. W. LEADBEATER.   Cloth, 35 cents.

No. 6.
THE DEVACHANIC PLANE.

By C. W. LEADBEATER.   Cloth, 35 cents.

No. 7.
MAN AND HIS BODIES.

By ANNIE BESANT.   Cloth, 35 cents.

FOR SALE BY

Mercury Pub. Office, 414 Mason St., San Francisco,

——OR——

Theosophical Publishing Society,

65 Fifth Avenue,   New York City.

A Systematic Course of Reading in Theosophy.

ELEMENTARY.

An Introduction to Theosophy, by Annie Besant........ $	.10
The Seven Principles of Man, by Annie Besant..........	.35
Re-incarnation, by Annie Besant......................	.35
Death and After, by Annie Besant.....................	.35
Karma, by Annie Besant..............................	.35
The Astral Plane, by C. W. Leadbeater................	.35
The Devachanic Plane, by C. W. Leadbeater...........	.35
Man and His Bodies, by Annie Besant..................	.35
The Ancient Wisdom, an Outline of Theosophical Teachings, by Annie Besant (in preparation).............	1.50
The Key to Theosophy, by H. P. Blavatsky.............	1.50
Theosophical Essays, by Annie Besant.................	.75

ADVANCED.

Esoteric Buddhism, by A. P. Sinnett...................	1.25
The Growth of the Soul, by A. P. Sinnett.............	1.50
The Building of the Kosmos, by Annie Besant..........	.75
The Self and Its Sheaths, by Annie Besant............	.50
The Birth and Evolution of the Soul, by Annie Besant...	.35
Plotinus (Theosophy of the Greeks), by G. R. S. Mead..	.35
Orpheus (Theosophy of the Greeks), by G. R. S. Mead..	1.25
The Secret Doctrine, by H. P. Blavatsky..............	12.50
Isis Unveiled, by H. P. Blavatsky.....	7.50

ETHICAL.

The Voice of the Silence. Translated by H. P. Blavatsky. Paper 15 cents, cloth 75 cents, leather..............	1.00
The Bhagavad Gita. Translated by Annie Besant. Paper 15 cents, cloth 50 cents, leather....................	1.00
The Upanishads (twelve—in two vols.). Translated by G. R. S. Mead and Jagadisha C. Chattopadhyaya. Paper, 15 cents each; cloth, each....................	.50
Light on the Path, by M. C............................	.40
In the Outer Court, by Annie Besant..................	.75
The Path of Discipleship, by Annie Besant............	.75
First Steps in Occultism, by H. P. Blavatsky. Cloth 50 cents, leather................................	1.00

FOR SALE BY

Theosophical Publishing Society,

65 Fifth Avenue,   New York City.

The Human Aura

—BY—

A. MARQUES,

PRESIDENT ALOHA BRANCH T. S.

A fascinating study in occult research, showing something of the marvels the higher vision unfolds to the student, and giving a method for development of the higher vision.

Illustrated with colored diagrams.

PRICE, PAPER 40C, CLOTH 70C.

Printed and for sale by

Mercury Publishing Office,

414 MASON ST.,   SAN FRANCISCO, CAL.

www.ingramcontent.com/pod-product-compliance
Lightning Source LLC
Chambersburg PA
CBHW030838270326
41928CB00007B/1107